HOT TOPICS

Hands-on activities ● Investigations ● Model-making ... and much more!

Dinosaurs

ages
5–11
for all primary years

Peter Riley

Author
Peter Riley

Editor
Roanne Charles

Assistant Editor
Niamh O'Carroll

Cover and inside illustrations
Laszlo Veres/Beehive Illustration

Photocopiable page illustrations
Ray and Corinne Burrows

Back cover and inside photography
Peter Rowe

Model-making
Linda Jones.

Polaroid photos
Linda Jones. Except pages 17, 24 (right), 27, 40 (bottom), 42, 57 and 75, Peter Rowe.

Series Designer
Helen Taylor

Cover concept/designer
Helen Taylor

Text © 2007 Peter Riley

© 2007 Scholastic Ltd

Designed using Adobe InDesign

Published by Scholastic Ltd
Villiers House
Clarendon Avenue
Leamington Spa
Warwickshire CV32 5PR

www.scholastic.co.uk

Printed by Tien Wah, Singapore.
1 2 3 4 5 6 7 8 9   7 8 9 0 1 2 3 4 5 6

British Library Cataloguing-in-Publication Data
A catalogue record for this book is available from the British Library.

ISBN 978-0439-94509-7

The rights of the author Peter Riley have been asserted in accordance with the Copyright, Designs and Patents Act 1988.

Crown copyright material is reproduced under the terms of the Click Use Licence.

The publishers gratefully acknowledge:
Early Learning Centre for the use of dinosaur models for photography.
Everything Dinosaur for images and models used for some of the photographs in this book © Everything Dinosaur (**www.everythingdinosaur.com**).

Contents

IMAGE © MMAGALLAN, STOCK.XCHNG

Introduction

The *Hot Topics* series explores topics that can be taught across the curriculum. Each book divides its topic into a number of themes that can be worked through progressively to build up a firm foundation of knowledge and provide opportunities for developing a wide range of skills. Each theme provides background information and three lesson plans, for ages 5–7, 7–9 and 9–11. Each lesson plan looks at a different aspect of the theme and varies in complexity from a simple approach with younger children to a more complex approach with older children. There are also photocopiable pages to support the lessons in each theme.

BACKGROUND INFORMATION

Each theme starts by providing information to support you in teaching the lesson. You may share it with the children as part of your own lesson plan or use it to help answer some the children's questions as they arise. Information is given about the material on the photocopiable sheets as well as the answers to any questions which have been set. This section also provides a brief overview of all three lessons to help you select content for your own sessions.

The lessons

A detailed structure is provided for lessons aimed at children who are in the 7–9 age range. Less detailed plans, covering all the essentials, are given for the lessons aimed at the other two age ranges, so covering the entire primary age range.

Detailed lesson plans

The detailed lesson plans have the following format:

Objectives

The content of all lesson plans is focused on specific objectives related to the study of dinosaurs.

Subject references

All lesson plans show how they relate to specific curriculum-related objectives. These objectives are based on statements in the National Curriculum in England. They may be used as they are, or regarded as an illustration of the statements that may be addressed, helping you to find others which you consider more appropriate for your needs.

Resources and preparation

This section lists everything you will need to deliver the lesson, including any photocopiables provided in this book. Preparation describes anything that needs to be done in advance of the lesson, for example cutting up cardboard dinosaur bones. As part of the preparation you should consult your school's policies on all practical work so that you can select activities for which you are confident to take responsibility. The ASE publication *Be Safe!* (ISBN 0-863-57324-X) gives useful guidance for conducting safe science activities.

Starter

A Starter is only provided in the more detailed lesson plans for ages 7–9. It provides an introduction to the lesson, helping the children to focus on the topic and generate interest.

What to do

This section sets out, point by point, the sequence of activities in the main part of the lesson. It may include activities for you to do, but concentrates mainly on the children's work.

Differentiation

Differentiation is only provided in the more detailed lesson plans for ages 7–9. Suggestions are given for developing strategies for support and extension activities.

Assessment

This section is only provided in the lesson plans for the 7–9 age range. It suggests ways to assess children, either through the product of their work or through looking at how they performed in an activity.

Plenary

A Plenary is only provided in the lesson plans for the 7–9 age range. It shows how children can review their own work and assess their progress in learning about dinosaurs. It is not related to other lessons, but if you are planning a sequence of lessons you may also like to use it to generate interest in future dinosaur studies.

Outcomes

These are only provided in the lesson plans for the 7–9 age range. They relate to the general objectives. You may wish to add more specific outcomes related to the context in which you use the lesson.

Extension

This section is found in the lesson plans for 5–7 and 9–11 year olds. It allows you to take the initial content of the lesson further.

Flexibility and extra differentiation

As the lessons in each topic are clustered around a particular theme, you may wish to add parts of one lesson to parts of another. For example, in Theme 2, 'Dinosaur bones' you may choose to begin the 9–11 lesson about making a fossil with a demonstration of an activity from the 7–9 lesson about discovering dinosaur bones at different depths in the ground.

In the lesson plans for 7–9 year olds, differentiation is addressed directly with its own section. In lessons for the other age groups, differentiation is addressed by providing ideas for extension work. However, the themes are arranged so that you may also pick activities from the different age groups to provide differentiation. For example, in a lesson for ages 5–7 you may wish to add activities from the lesson for 7–9 year olds in the same theme.

Planning a project

Dinosaur Day: Ages 5–7
Preparation

• If appropriate, send a letter home asking for parents' and carers' help to make dinosaur costumes. If some children are unlikely to be able to bring a costume, collect some items that they could use.

• Invite the children to make the mask on page 62 (Theme 7 Lesson 2).
• Rehearse the song 'We are the dinosaurs' (photocopiable page 69).
• Encourage the children to bring in dinosaur models from home.

You may like to use the topic for a class or whole-school project culminating in a Dinosaur Day. This will need considerable preparation, but the result could be a very memorable event! This section provides some suggestions for activities leading up to the day and for a programme of events.

The suggested activities are featured in or based on the lesson plans shown in the third column. Read through each lesson plan to work out how the activity can fit into the context of your Dinosaur Day.

Times are given for guidance only. Depending on your circumstances, you might want to lengthen or shorten any activity.

Ages 5–7		Activity	Lesson plan	Pages
MORNING	15 minutes	Children show their dinosaur models	Looking at dinosaurs Theme 1 Lesson 1	9
	25 minutes	Construct a large table-top dinosaur habitat	Dinosaur world Theme 8 Lesson 1	65
	40 minutes	Find out about fossils	Digging up bones Theme 2 Lesson 1	17/21
	40 minutes	Make small fossil feet and lay tracks around the school	Dinosaur feet and tracks Theme 4 Lesson 1	32
	30 minutes	Discover how some dinosaurs stomachs worked	Grinding up food Theme 5 Lesson 2	41/45
AFTERNOON	40 minutes	Look at fossil eggs	Dinosaur eggs Theme 7 Lesson 1	57
	40 minutes	Explore what happened to the dinosaurs	Volcanoes and a space rock	74/78
	20 minutes	Final rehearsal and performance of the song	Dinosaur world Theme 8 Lesson 1	65/69

HOT TOPICS Dinosaurs

Dinosaur Day: ages 7–9
Preparation

- If appropriate, send a letter home asking for parents' help with costumes and so on.
- Show the children pictures of present-day palaeontologists and tell them that on Dinosaur Day they can dress up as dinosaur hunters (this means wearing shorts and hats).
- Rehearse the song 'We are the dinosaurs' on photocopiable page 69.
- Rehearse a dance based on the movements suggested by the children in Theme 8 Lesson 1, on page 65.

Dinosaur Day: ages 9–11
Preparation

- If appropriate, send a letter home asking for parents' help with costumes and so on.
- Show the children pictures of early dinosaur hunters. Many of them lived in Victorian times and you could link this with a Victorian Day.
- For part of the day the children could dress up in Victorian costumes. For children who might not be able to bring in a costume, collect items they could use.
- Tell the children that one scientist who studied dinosaurs had a big model made in which he and his friends could eat a meal. If possible, show pictures of Richard Owen in the dinosaur. Make one side of a dinosaur from cardboard, as explained on page 68 (Theme 8 Lesson 3).
- Provide details and pictures of Victorian meals for the children to write Victorian menus, as in Theme 8 Lesson 3 (page 68).
- You might like to select one or more activities from these suggestions or have different groups doing different activities.

Ages 7–9		Activity	Lesson plan	Pages
MORNING	40 minutes	Look for dinosaur bones and skeletons	Dinosaur skeletons Theme 2 Lesson 2	18/21
	40 minutes	Make a giant cardboard dinosaur	The size of a dinosaur Theme 3 Lesson 2	25/21/30
	40 minutes	Make dinosaur masks	Communicating with dinosaurs Theme 7 Lesson 2	58/62
	30 minutes	Discover how some dinosaurs' stomachs worked	Grinding up food Theme 5 Lesson 2	41/45
AFTERNOON	60 minutes	Make moving and noisy dinosaurs heads	Into attack Theme 6 Lesson 2	49/53
	40 minutes	Explore what happened to the dinosaurs	Volcanoes and a space rock	74/78
	30 minutes	Final rehearsal and performance of the song	Dinosaur times Theme 8 Lesson 2	65/69

Ages 9–11		Activity	Lesson plan	Pages
MORNING	40 minutes	Explore dinosaur skeletons	Dinosaur skeletons Theme 2 Lesson 2	18/21
	40 minutes	Look at different sizes of dinosaurs	The size of a dinosaur Theme 3 Lesson 2	25/30
	40 minutes	Make a fossil	Make a fossil Theme 2 Lesson 3	20/22
	40 minutes	Make large dinosaur footprints and lay a track around the school	Dinosaur tracks and speed Theme 4 Lesson 3	35
	15 minutes	Set up a giant dinosaur model and eat lunch inside	Discovering dinosaurs Theme 8 Lesson 3	68
AFTERNOON	60 minutes	Make moving and noisy dinosaur heads	Into attack Theme 6 Lesson 2	49/53
	40 minutes	Explore what happened to the dinosaurs	Volcanoes and a space rock	74/78
	40 minutes	Final out how it felt when dinosaur fossils were being discovered	Discovering dinosaurs Theme 8 Lesson 3	68/71

Introducing dinosaurs

BACKGROUND

There were many types of reptile living in the age of the dinosaurs, and dinosaurs were just one type. Most reptiles had limbs that grew out from the sides of their bodies like the limbs of the crocodiles today. Dinosaur limbs grew straight down under the body and this allowed them to move on land faster and further than other reptiles. This led to them reaching most land habitats and adapting to the conditions there.

THE CONTENTS

Lesson 1 (Ages 5–7)
Looking at dinosaurs

The children begin by identifying their model dinosaurs and distinguishing between them. They match up pictures of dinosaurs, and finish by thinking what it would be like to be a dinosaur, using mime.

Lesson 2 (Ages 7–9)
Grouping and classifying dinosaurs

The children begin by considering the groups of animals that are alive today and discover that the dinosaurs belong to the reptile group. They learn to distinguish dinosaurs from other reptiles that were alive at the same time and to put the dinosaurs into different groups.

Lesson 3 (Ages 9–11)
Design a dinosaur key

The children make a key to use for classifying and identifying dinosaurs.

Notes on photocopiables
Four dinosaurs (page 13)

The four dinosaurs shown on this page are:
A) Apatosaurus; B) Tyrannosaurus rex;
C) Triceratops; D) Stegosaurus.

Children might say that picture A is a Brontosaurus, but there is no longer a dinosaur called Brontosaurus. In 1877 a dinosaur was discovered and called Apatosaurus. In 1879 another dinosaur was discovered and called Brontosaurus. The Brontosaurus became more well known than the Apatosaurus. However, scientists then discovered that both were of the same species! There is a rule about naming dinosaurs that, if two dinosaurs are found to be the same, they must both take the name of the first specimen to be discovered. Therefore, as the first of the two to be discovered was named Apatosaurus, Brontosaurus is no longer used.

Spot the dinosaurs (page 14)

Not all the creatures here are dinosaurs. The dinosaurs are:
B (Nodosaurus); C (Tyrannosaurus rex);
F (Triceratops); G (Kentrosaurus);
H (Ceratosaurus); I (Diplodocus);
K (Ankylosaurus); L (Brachiosaurus);
M (Pentaceratops); P (Stegosaurus).

The other animals are:
A and D (pterosaurs); E and J (plesiosaurs); N and O (ichthyosaurs).

The dinosaurs can also be sorted into five groups, as follows:
Group 1– bands of lumps on back (B and K);
Group 2 – very short front legs (C and H);
Group 3 – horns on their heads (F and M);
Group 4 – plates and spines on back and tail (G and P);
Group 5 – long necks and tails (I and L).

A dinosaur key (page 15)

Long neck: Group 5 – I and L;
Short front legs: Group 2 – C and H;
Horns: Group 3 – F and M;
Bands of lumps on back: Group 1 – B and K;
Plates and spines down back and tail: Group 4 – G and P.

HOT TOPICS Dinosaurs

Lesson 1 Looking at dinosaurs

Resources and preparation
- Ask the children to bring in model dinosaurs from home.
- Make enlarged copies of the pictures on 'Four dinosaurs', page 13.
- Photocopy and cut out the pictures from 'Spot the dinosaurs', page 14 (two sets per pair or group). Discard pictures A, D, E, J, N and O (or keep for the extension activity). Mix up the remaining pictures and put them all in a large envelope.
- This lesson can be adapted to be part of your Dinosaur Day.

What to do
- Show the children the pictures from 'Four dinosaurs' and see if they can match their model dinosaurs with the pictures. Encourage them to identify the dinosaurs.
- Give the children the envelopes which contains the pictures from the 'Spot the dinosaurs' sheets and ask them to match up the pictures of the dinosaurs, as if they are playing 'Pairs'.
- Ask the children to consider what it might have been like to be dinosaur A

(Apatosaurus) from the 'Four dinosaurs' sheet. Invite them to mime being this dinosaur by making their right arm a head and long neck, and their left arm a tail. Encourage them to stamp around the classroom! They could then think about and mime dinosaur B (Tyrannosaurus rex) by holding up their arms under their chests, opening their mouths wide to show their teeth, and roaring. The children could mime dinosaur C (Triceratops) by putting their hands to their head to make horns.
- Now challenge the children to think how they could represent dinosaur D (Stegosaurus). Suggest the possibility of sticking triangular pieces of stiff card to their backs. This could lead to thinking about what could go into making a dinosaur costume.

Extension
Give the children the remaining pictures from the 'Spot the dinosaurs' sheet and ask them if they think they are dinosaurs. As a clue, tell the children that dinosaurs only lived on land.

Did you know?
Diplodocus and Tyrannosaurus have lizard-shaped hips and Stegosaurus and Triceratops have bird-shaped hips.

PHOTOGRAPH © PETER ROWE. MODEL DINOSAURS © HELEN TAYLOR

Lesson 2 Grouping and classifying dinosaurs

Resources and preparation
● Photocopy page 13, 'Four dinosaurs', large enough to show to the class and/or to give one to each group.
● Make copies of page 14, 'Spot the dinosaurs', for each group or individual.

Starter
● Ask the children if they can think of any groups of animals. Look for answers that include mammals, birds and reptiles. See if the children can name and describe any reptiles.
● Tell the children that dinosaurs belonged to the reptile group and lived millions of years ago. Nobody was around to see them and the ideas we have today about how they looked have come from the bones they left behind when they died, which have become fossils.
● Show the children the 'Four dinosaurs' sheet and ask them to name each of the dinosaurs.
● To help to illustrate the difference that dinosaurs' leg positions made compared to other reptiles, ask the children to lie face-down on the floor and get in the position to do a press-up. When the children do this, ask them to notice that their arms are sticking out from the side of their bodies. Encourage the children to raise their bodies by pushing their arms, and then hold that position. Do they have to use a lot of energy to hold their bodies up? Now ask them to drop back down gently and instead be dinosaurs by putting their arms straight under their bodies to raise themselves up. They should realise that it is easier to keep their bodies raised in this position. Emphasise that dinosaurs were land animals and having their limbs beneath them was best for this environment.

What to do
● Give the children the 'Spot the dinosaurs' sheet and ask them to identify which of the pictures show dinosaurs. They could either write down the letter of each dinosaur or cut out all the pictures and put the dinosaurs into one group.
● Now ask the children to sort the dinosaurs into five different groups, numbered 1–5, and to give reasons for the way they have grouped the animals. When they have finished sorting the dinosaur cards, invite the class to share their findings.

Check their responses with the groupings given in Notes on photocopiables, under 'Spot the dinosaurs', on page 8.

Differentiation
● Give less confident learners pairs of pictures, showing one dinosaur and one non-dinosaur, and ask them to select the dinosaur in each pair.
● More confident learners can be given reference books and asked to identify some of the dinosaurs on the sheet.

Assessment
During the activity, go around the class and ask the children how they are deciding which animals are not dinosaurs. Look for answers about animals that do not live on land, but live either in the air or in water. Some children may need help in spotting that E and J (plesiosaurs) have flippers and are not like I and L.

Plenary
● Remind the children that dinosaurs only lived on land and ask them to tell you about where the other reptiles on the sheet lived. They should be able to point out that A and D (pterosaurs) lived in the air and that E, J, N and O (plesiosaurs and ichthyosaurs) lived in water.
● Ask them about how dinosaurs' bodies varied, and look for answers about variation in neck length, leg length and in body armour.
● Talk about the value of organising different types of animal into groups, and look for understanding about classification making dinosaurs easier to study. Clarify this by saying that palaeontologists (scientists who study fossil animals like dinosaurs) group dinosaurs in the same way as grouping animals into mammals, birds and reptiles makes them easier to study. For example, G and P (with plates along their spines) belong to a group called the stegosaurids, while F and M (with horns) belong to a group called the ceratopsids.

Outcome
The children can distinguish dinosaurs from other reptiles and describe their range of forms.

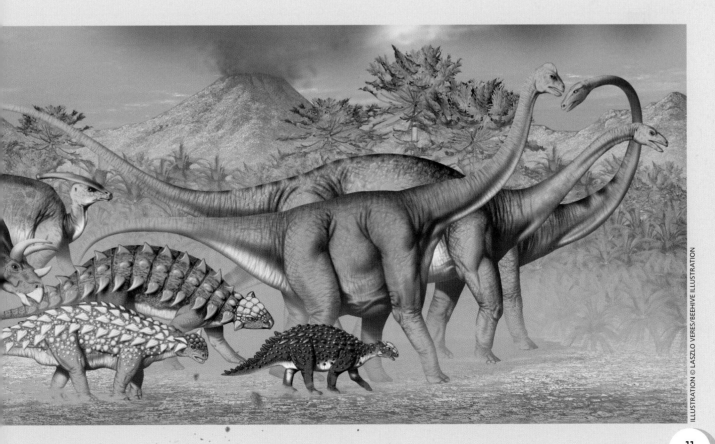

Lesson 3 Design a dinosaur key

AGES 9-11

Objectives
● To construct a key.
● To make modifications to the key in the light of research.

Subject references
Science
● Make and use a key. (NC: KS2 Sc2 4a)

Resources and preparation
● Make copies of page 14, 'Spot the dinosaurs' and page 15, 'A dinosaur key' so you have one of each for each child.
● Provide information books containing pictures of dinosaurs (including Gallimimus).
● The children will need scissors.

What to do
● Give each of the children a copy of the 'Spot the dinosaurs' sheet and let them cut out the pictures. Ask them to select which pictures are the dinosaurs and then to sort the dinosaurs into five different groups numbered from 1–5. Check the children's choices against the answers given in Notes on photocopiables, under 'Spot the dinosaurs', on page 8.
● Now ask the children to construct a key in the form of a tree diagram, into which each of the groups can be fitted. Explain that in a key like this, a question is asked to which there are usually just two possible answers. Therefore, the key could be started by asking the question: *Do they have long necks or short necks?* The children would then find that they have one group (for example, group 5) on its own under 'Long necks' and all the other groups under 'Short necks'. Help the children to continue asking themselves questions until the key is complete. Check their answers by showing them the sheet 'A dinosaur key'.
● Alternatively, give each child a copy of 'A dinosaur key' and ask them to arrange the dinosaurs on it.

Extension
Let the children look through information books on dinosaurs to test their key against the pictures shown there. Help them to revise the key to take into account any dinosaur shapes that they think do not fit it. For example, they may consider that Gallimimus has a long neck and tail and has two short front legs.

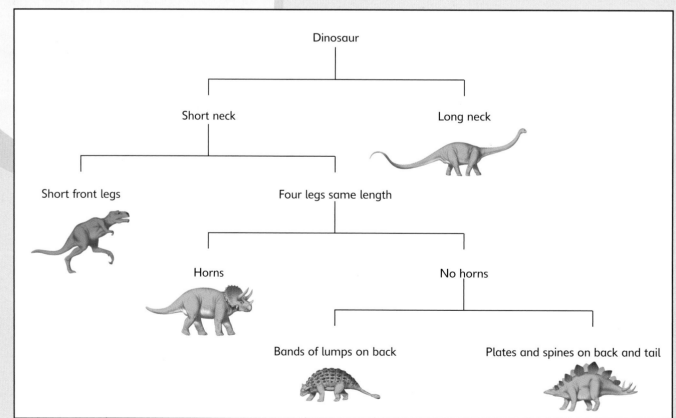

Theme 1 Four dinosaurs

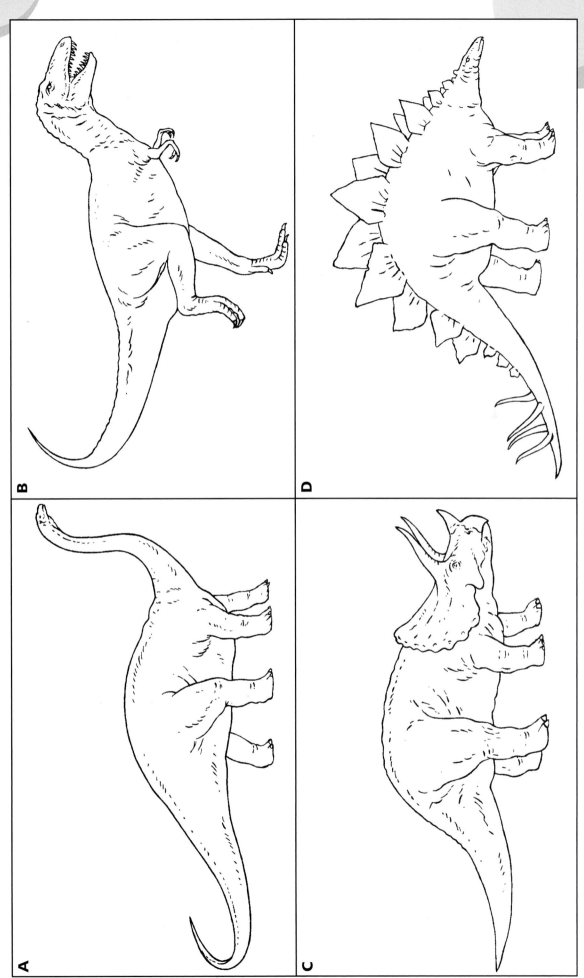

Theme 1 Spot the dinosaurs

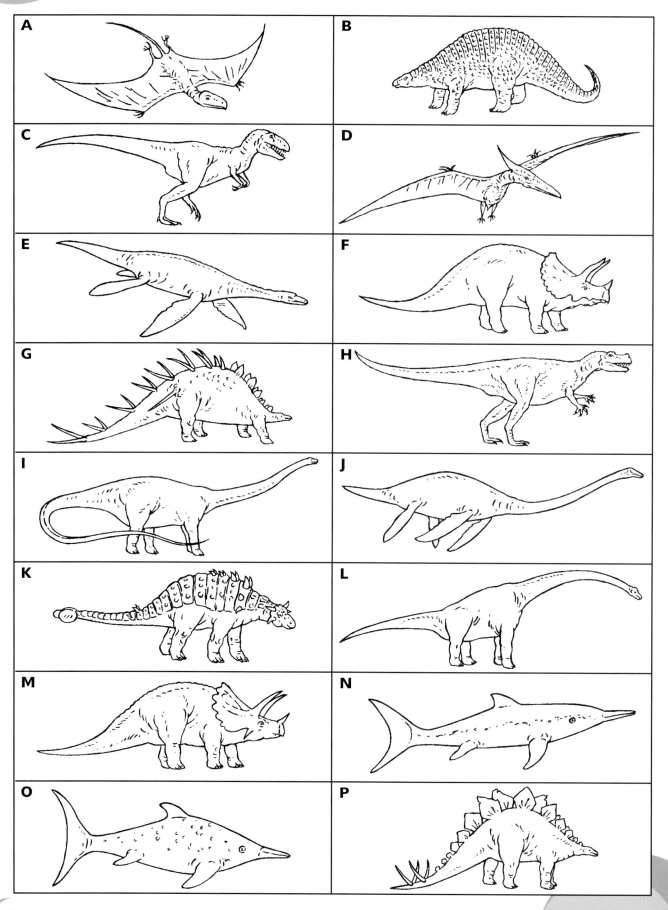

Theme 1 A dinosaur key

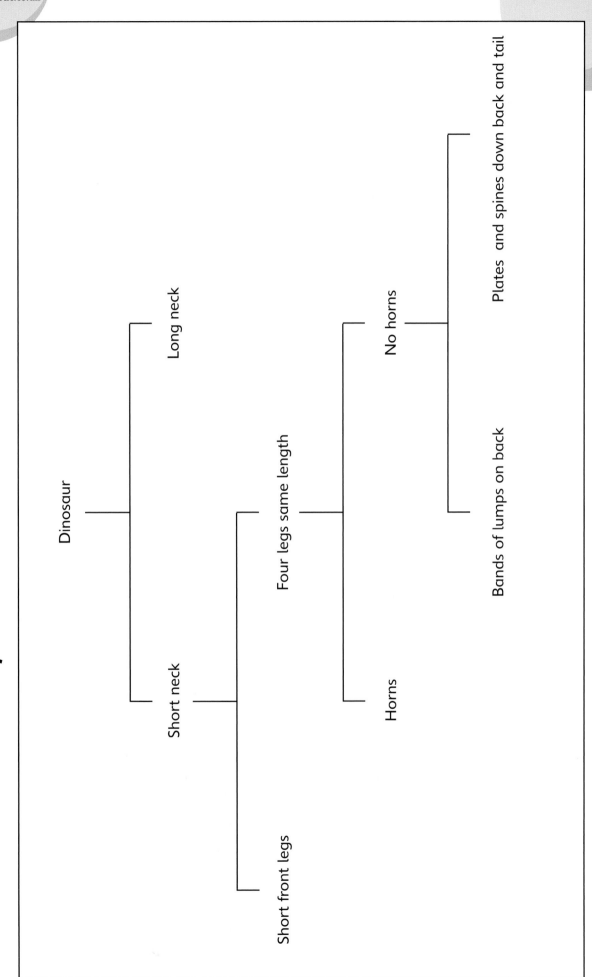

Dinosaur

Long neck

Short neck

Four legs same length

Short front legs

Horns

No horns

Plates and spines down back and tail

Bands of lumps on back

Dinosaur bones

BACKGROUND

When most dinosaurs died, their bodies were eaten by other dinosaurs. Occasionally a dinosaur's body became covered with mud before it could be eaten. When this happened, the flesh decayed and over time the bones turned into fossils. In one form of fossilisation, the material in the bones was replaced by minerals in water that was running through the ground and the bones turned to stone. In another kind, the bones were dissolved by the water and a hollow was left. In time, this hollow filled up with minerals from the water passing through it.

The age of dinosaurs is divided into three parts:
- The Triassic (225–213 million years ago)
- The Jurassic (213–144 million years)
- The Cretaceous (114–65 million years ago).

As the dinosaur bones turned to fossils, the mud around them turned into rock. The fossils formed in layers of sedimentary rock like sandstone and limestone. The layers of rock formed at different times, generally with the older rocks being lower in the ground than the younger ones.

Most dinosaur bones have to be chipped very carefully out of the rock around them. Sometimes bones can be dug out of the sand in deserts.

THE CONTENTS
Lesson 1 (Ages 5–7)
Digging up bones
The children learn how to excavate 'bones' by carefully removing sand from over them. They discover how difficult it is to assemble the bones to make a skeleton.

Lesson 2 (Ages 7–9)
Dinosaur skeletons
The children excavate 'bones' from different depths of sand to appreciate that fossil dinosaur skeletons formed over a long period of time. They discover the value in carefully removing the bones so that bones from different skeletons do not get mixed up. They discover that assembling a skeleton can be difficult.

Lesson 3 (Ages 9–11)
Make a fossil
The children discover how a copy of a hard object can be made by forming a hollow and filling it with a second material. This process occurs when many fossils are made.

Notes on photocopiables
Dinosaur skeleton (page 21)
The dinosaur skeletons shows on this page are:
A) Tyrannosaurus rex (Cretaceous)
B) Cetiosauriscus (Jurassic)
C) Plateosaurus (Triassic).

These dinosaurs also belong to the following groups from the five dinosaur groups in Theme 1 Lesson 2 'Grouping and classifying dinosaurs':
A) Tyrannosaurus rex (Group 2 – very short front legs)
B) Cetiosauriscus (Group 5 – long necks and tails)
C) Plateosaurus (Group 2 – very short front legs).

Make a fossil (page 22)
This sheet provides simple instructions and diagrams for making a plaster-cast fossil.

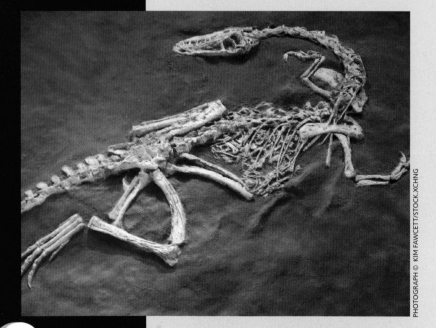

PHOTOGRAPH © KIM FAWCETT/STOCK.XCHNG

HOTTOPICS Dinosaurs

Lesson 1 Digging up bones

Resources and preparation
● Photocopy page 21, 'Dinosaur skeletons', onto stiff white, cream or yellow card. Cut out each dinosaur and then cut each one into four to six pieces.
● Place some sand in a dish for each dinosaur. Spread out the pieces of card on the sand and then cover with more sand. Provide two spoons for each dish of dinosaur bones. Place each dish in a tray.
● Provide a complete picture of each dinosaur skeleton from page 21 for reference.
● This lesson can be adapted to be part of your Dinosaur Day.

What to do
● Tell the children that they are going to be dinosaur hunters who dig in sand for dinosaur bones. Show them the dishes of dinosaur bones and encourage them to 'excavate' the bones carefully by removing sand gently with a spoon. As they dig, they should empty the spoons of sand into the tray. When they have removed the sand from around some of the bones, they should carefully lift them onto the table.
● When all the groups of bones have been collected, ask the children to try to assemble them to make a dinosaur. They can compare the groups of bones with the picture to help them assemble the skeleton, or they can try to assemble the skeleton and then check the picture.

Extension
● Give each child a complete copy of 'Dinosaur skeletons' and explain that the shape of the 'living' dinosaur can be found by drawing round the outline of the skeleton. Ask the children to do this.
● If the children have completed Theme 1 Lesson 2 'Grouping and classifying dinosaurs' (page 10), remind them of the five dinosaur groups and ask them to decide in which group each dinosaur belongs. Check their answers with those given in Notes on photocopiables, under 'Dinosaur skeletons', on page 16.

PHOTOGRAPH © PETER ROWE

AGES 5–7

Objectives
● To use equipment safely and carefully.
● To make observations on bones and assemble them into a skeleton.

Subject references
Science
● Follow simple instructions to control the risks to themselves and others.
(NC: KS1 Sc1 2e)

Lesson 2 Dinosaur skeletons

AGES 7–9

Objectives
● To use equipment safely and carefully.
● To make observations on bones and assemble them into skeletons.
● To make comparisons between similar bones from different dinosaurs.

Subject references
Science
● Use simple equipment and materials appropriately and take action to control risks.
(NC: KS2 Sc1 2e)

Resources and preparation
● Photocopy page 21, 'Dinosaur skeletons', onto stiff white, cream or yellow card. Cut out each dinosaur and then cut each one in the following way (you can cut them up into larger pieces if you wish):
1. Cut off the head, the neck, the portion of backbone and shoulder blade at the top of the front legs.
2. Cut the front leg into two at the elbow.
3. Cut the backbone and ribs, and the pelvis, (note there are parts of the pelvis in front and behind the upper part of the hind limb).
4. Cut the hind limb into two at the knee.
● Prepare either a box of sand and bones for each group in the class, or just prepare one box and use it in a demonstration in which children can help. Place some sand in the bottom of a plastic box or deep tray, and then lay the bones of dinosaur C (Plateosaurus) on it. Cover the bones with sand to a depth of three centimetres, then place the bones of dinosaur B (Cetiosauriscus) on it. Cover the bones with another three centimetres of sand, and place the bones of dinosaur A (Tyrannosaurus) on it. Cover these bones with a layer of sand one centimetre deep.
● Provide two spoons for each box and a large tray per box into which the sand can be placed as the children dig down.
● This lesson can be adapted to be part of your Dinosaur Day.

Starter
Tell the children that most of the information we have about dinosaurs comes from the bones they left behind. You could also tell them about how fossils are formed, as explained in the Background section on page 16.

What to do
● Show the children the sand trays and explain that there are bones buried in the sand. Say that you would like them to remove the bones carefully and then store them in a safe place.
● Explain that there might be bones found at different levels in the sand and that care must be taken when digging, so as not to mix up the bones from different levels.
● When the bones have been collected from each level, invite the groups or class to work together to identify the different bone sections and to assemble each set into a skeleton.

Differentiation
● Give children who need support a copy of the complete skeleton of the dinosaur from page 21 to help them place the bones in the correct positions.
● More confident learners could try to assemble the skeleton without the use of the picture.

PHOTOGRAPH © BWK, STOCK.XCHNG

Did you know?
Large dinosaurs had hollows in their backbones to make them lighter and able to move more easily.

Assessment

The children can be assessed for the way they carefully removed the bones, and assembled the skeletons, with or without help.

Plenary

Encourage the children to glue the pieces of skeleton onto paper and then ask them to find out the shape of the dinosaur. If the children have completed Theme 1 Lesson 2, 'Grouping and classifying dinosaurs', remind them of the five dinosaur groups and ask them to decide to which group each dinosaur belongs. Check their answers with those given in Notes on photocopiables, under 'Dinosaur skeletons', on page 16.

Outcomes

- The children can carefully remove dinosaur bones from sand.
- They can assemble the bones into skeletons.
- They can relate the position of the bones to the shape of the dinosaur's body.

Lesson 3 Make a fossil

PHOTOGRAPH © SASAN, STOCK.XCHNG

Resources and preparation
• Provide each group with a five-centimetre cube of Plasticine.
• Provide each group with a small hard item, such as a small marine shell (for example a periwinkle) or a small bone-shaped object made from self-hardening modelling clay.
• Provide a plastic knife, and a dish in which you have mixed plaster of Paris and water to a creamy constituency. This will need to be made when the children have made their moulds.
• Make copies of page 22, 'Make a fossil', for all of the children.
• Set up a box of sand filled with cut-out dinosaur bones from photocopiable page 21, 'Dinosaur bones', as described in the preparation for Lesson 2, 'Dinosaur skeletons' (see page 18 for details).
• Provide reference materials for further research on dinosaur fossils.

What to do
• Show the children the sand boxes and tell them that there are bones buried in the sand that you would like them to remove carefully and store in a safe place.

• Explain that there might be bones found at different levels in the sand so care must be taken when digging to ensure that bones from different levels are not mixed up.
• When the bones have been collected from each level, ask the class or groups to work together to assemble each one into a skeleton.
• Next, give each child a copy of 'Make a fossil' and read through the sheet together.
• Ask the children to carry out steps 1–3, following the instructions on the photocopiable sheet.
• When the children reach step 4, begin to mix the water and plaster of Paris and then let the children pour it carefully into the holes of their moulds.
• When you are sure the plaster has set, encourage the children to carry out step 5. Emphasise that they should do this very carefully. The children will find that they have made a plaster cast of the object they pressed into the Plasticine.

Extension
Invite the children to use secondary sources to find out what other kinds of dinosaur fossils formed beside bones (for example, eggs, skin, tracks and droppings).

Theme 2 Dinosaur skeletons

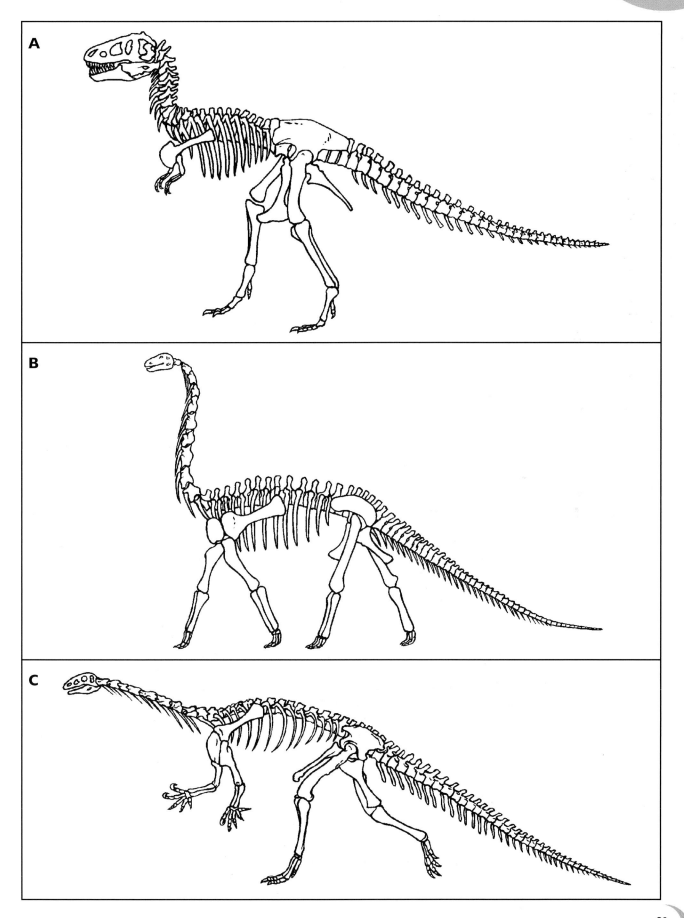

A

B

C

Theme 2 Make a fossil

1. Cut a Plasticine block in half, using a plastic knife.

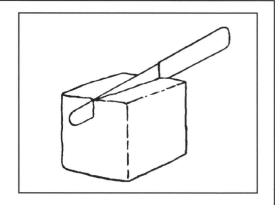

2. Place a shell or bone-shaped object between the two halves of the Plasticine block and press the halves together so an indentation of the object is left in the Plasticine.

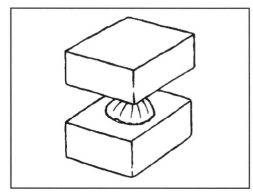

3. Cut out grooves going to the hollows made by the object in the Plasticine halves.

4. Pour a mixture of plaster of Paris into the hole and leave to set.

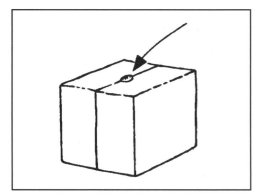

5. When the plaster has set completely, remove the block. What do you find?

Dinosaur bodies

BACKGROUND

Nobody has ever seen a real dinosaur body. Our ideas about dinosaurs' bodies are built up from the bones in their skeletons. When their bodies have been examined they have been found to have many features in common with human bodies. For example, 'Parts of a dinosaur' on page 28 shows Troodon. Troodon had a large brain for a dinosaur and eyes that pointed forward so that it had binocular vision, like humans, and was able to judge distances accurately. Its legs and feet, however, were more like those of a bird. The hind part of the foot is raised up to make a joint with the lower leg at a place where we would expect the knee to be. The knee is much higher up.

The length of a dinosaur body is the feature usually mentioned in measurements, although the height might also be given. The mass (usually written as the weight) is also often given. You might not want to distinguish mass (the amount of matter in a substance and measured in kilograms) and weight (the force of a body pushing down on the Earth and measured in newtons), but explain that in everyday life, objects are 'weighed' in kilograms but this represents the mass of the object or the amount of matter in it. This mass (weight) of a dinosaur is worked out by using scale models, assuming the mass (weight) of dinosaur flesh is the same as alligator flesh (as explained in 'The weight of a dinosaur' on page 27).

THE CONTENTS

Lesson 1 (Ages 5–7)
Parts of the body
The children compare their own body with a dinosaur and discover similarities and differences. They find out that the length of the neck is counterbalanced by a long tail.

Lesson 2 (Ages 7–9)
The size of a dinosaur
The children work out the size of a dinosaur from a few 'bones'. They compare it with the sizes of other dinosaurs.

Lesson 3 (Ages 9–11)
The weight of a dinosaur
The children discover how scientists work out the weight of dinosaurs from scale models.

Notes on photocopiables
Parts of a dinosaur (page 28)
The body of this dinosaur can be labelled in a similar way to a human body. Ensure that you share the background information regarding the ankle and knee, as the bone arrangement is similar to a bird.

Necks and tails (page 29)
When the children make models of dinosaur B and dinosaur C, the models will fall over. (Some children may make models of dinosaur A that fall over too.) They will find that when they make models of dinosaurs D, E and F the models will not fall over because the tail will balance the weight of the dinosaur.

Dinosaur leg bones (page 30)
This represents the back leg of the Cetiosauriscus. See 'Dinosaur skeletons' on page 21 for an illustration of the full skeleton.

PHOTOGRAPH © XAMERON, STOCK.XCHNG

Lesson 1 Parts of the body

AGES 5–7

Objectives
● To compare parts of the human body with a dinosaur body.
● To understand what it is to balance.
● To understand why some dinosaurs had long necks and long tails.

Subject references
Science
● Follow simple instructions to control the risks to themselves and others.
(NC: KS1 Sc1 2e)
● Make simple comparisons and identify simple associations.
(NC: KS1 Sc1 2h)
● Recognise and compare the main external parts of the bodies of humans and other animals.
(NC: KS1 Sc2 2a)

Resources and preparation
● Make copies of page 28, 'Parts of a dinosaur' and page 29, 'Necks and tails'.
● Provide glue, scissors and a large lump of Plasticine for each child.

What to do
● Give out copies of 'Parts of a dinosaur' and ask the children to look closely at the body-part labels. Can they find and point to these parts of the body on themselves?
● Invite the children to cut out the label boxes and glue the labels near the appropriate part on the dinosaur, and draw a key-line to it.
● Ask the children to examine and write down the ways in which the dinosaur head is similar to their own, and the ways in which it is different.
● Next, give each child a copy of 'Necks and tails' and a lump of Plasticine. Ask them why some dinosaurs had long necks. Look for an answer about being able to reach food high up in the trees.
● Encourage the children to think about why the dinosaurs also had long tails. Some children may say that they swept them from side to side to sweep attackers away, or that some dinosaurs could sit back on their tails to reach higher into the trees.

Both these answers could be true, but look particularly for an answer about the tail helping the dinosaur to keep its balance and stop its long neck toppling it forwards. Develop this idea by asking the children to predict which dinosaurs in the pictures on 'Necks and tails' would not balance easily.
● Let the children make model dinosaurs from Plasticine, following the designs on the photocopiable sheet, to test their predictions.

Extension
Develop the idea of balance by asking the children to stand on one leg and keep their arms by their sides. They should wobble over and lose their balance fairly quickly. Now ask them to put out their arms; they should balance more easily. This activity produces faster results if the children close their eyes!

ILLUSTRATION © LASZLO VERES/BEEHIVE ILLUSTRATION

Lesson 2 The size of a dinosaur

PHOTOGRAPH © DEREK COOKNELL

AGES 7–9

Objectives
● To appreciate the size of dinosaurs.
● To estimate sizes of dinosaurs from model bones.
● To measure the size of a dinosaur body.

Subject references
Mathematics
● Make sensible estimates.
(NC: KS2 Ma3 4a)
● Choose suitable measuring instruments for a task.
(NC: KS2 Ma3 4b)

Resources and preparation
● Make an A3 copy of page 30, 'Dinosaur leg bones', for each child.
● Make a large reference copy of the Cetiosauriscus skeleton from 'Dinosaur skeletons' on page 21.
● Provide an ordinary ruler, a metre rule, some wallpaper or lining paper, fat felt-tipped pens and child scissors for each group.
● You will need a large space such as the school hall.
● This lesson can be adapted to be part of your Dinosaur Day.

Starter
● Remind the children that the main evidence scientists have been able to collect about dinosaur bodies comes from their bones. Explain that sometimes a full skeleton is not found and the scientists have to work out the size, and sometimes the shape, of the dinosaur from just a few bones. They can do this if they know where the bones fit in the skeleton.
● Tell the children that they are going to estimate the size of a dinosaur from a few bones, and that they will have a picture of a complete dinosaur skeleton to help them.

What to do
● Let the children cut out the leg bones from the photocopiable sheet and lay them on the floor, as if they had found them at a dinosaur dig.
● Tell the children that the bones are from the back leg of Cetiosauriscus. Show the children the picture of the whole skeleton of a Cetiosauriscus so they can understand more clearly where the bones are from.
● Ask the children to estimate the size of the body, tail, head and neck of the Cetiosauriscus, and to make drawings of these regions on wallpaper. Remind them to refer to the picture of the whole skeleton to help them with positions and relative sizes. Set out the drawings on the floor to see how big the dinosaur would have been.
● Tell the children that a full-sized Cetiosauriscus was 18 metres long. Let them measure out this distance and compare it with the length of the dinosaur they have made.

ILLUSTRATIONS © WWW.EVERYTHINGDINOSAUR.COM

Did you know?

A Brachiosaurus' forelimbs were longer than it's hind limbs.

PHOTOGRAPH © BARRETO, STOCK.XCHNG

Differentiation

● Some children may need help to make the drawings on the wallpaper and will need an adult to assist with the measurement and estimating.

● Extend children by giving them the following body lengths of adult dinosaurs, and asking them to measure them out and think about what the dinosaur skeletons would look like: Tyrannosaurus – 12m; Plateosaurus – 8m; Troodon – 2m; Ultrasaurus (a much larger version of Cetiosauriscus) – 25m.

Assessment

The children can be assessed by the estimates they make for the size of the dinosaur body and for the accuracy in measuring out the dinosaur bodies.

Plenary

● Ask the children to arrange certain dinosaurs in order of size, starting with the dinosaur they have just made. Explain, for example, that Troodon is about the size of a tall human adult. Riojasaurus was similar to Cetiosauriscus, but it was 11 metres long (about the length of a bus).

● Suggest to the children that if they want to imagine the size of a large dinosaur moving down a street they should think of a bus. Next time they are at a bus station they should think of the buses as dinosaurs to get an impression of what a herd of large dinosaurs might have been like!

Outcomes

● The children can appreciate the size of dinosaurs.

● They can make accurate measurements and realistic estimations.

Lesson 3 The weight of a dinosaur

Resources and preparation
- You will need scale-model dinosaurs, measuring cylinders and string.
- Prepare tanks or bowls of water, large enough to hold the scale models, placed on trays (to contain overspill).
- Provide reference information giving the lengths of common dinosaurs.

What to do
- Tell the children that scientists assume that the weight of a volume of dinosaur flesh is the same as the weight of a volume of alligator flesh. One litre of alligator flesh has a mass of 0.9kg. Scientists use this fact to work out the weight of a dinosaur by the method described here.
- Tell the children that you are going to find out the volume of the scale-model dinosaur by placing it in a tank or bowl, which is stood on a tray and filled to the brim with water.
- Show the children how to lower the scale-model dinosaur into the water on a string until the model is completely covered in water. While this is happening, water will flow into the tray.
- Remove the model dinosaur and use a measuring cylinder to top up the water level again. The volume of water replaced is the same as the volume of the scale model.

- Tell the children that to find the volume of the actual dinosaur, they need to multiply the volume of the model by its scale. For example, a model dinosaur with a volume of 200cm³, which is 20 times smaller than the actual dinosaur, gives a volume for the real dinosaur of 200 × 20 = 4000cm³.
- Now they have found the volume of the dinosaur, the children can move on to finding its weight. This is found by multiplying the volume of the actual dinosaur in litres with the weight of a litre of flesh (0.9kg). For example, the dinosaur with a volume of 4000cm³ has a volume of 40 litres (1 litre = 1000cm³) so its actual weight is 40 × 0.9 = 36kg.
- Invite the children to find the volumes of some common models of dinosaurs. The scale of the models can be worked out roughly by measuring the length of the model and comparing it with the lengths given for common dinosaurs. For example, a Tyrannosaurus is 1400cm, a Brachiosaurus is 2500cm, a Stegosaurus 900cm and a Triceratops 900cm.

Extension
Encourage the children to use secondary sources to find the smallest and largest dinosaurs that ever existed.

Theme 3 Parts of a dinosaur

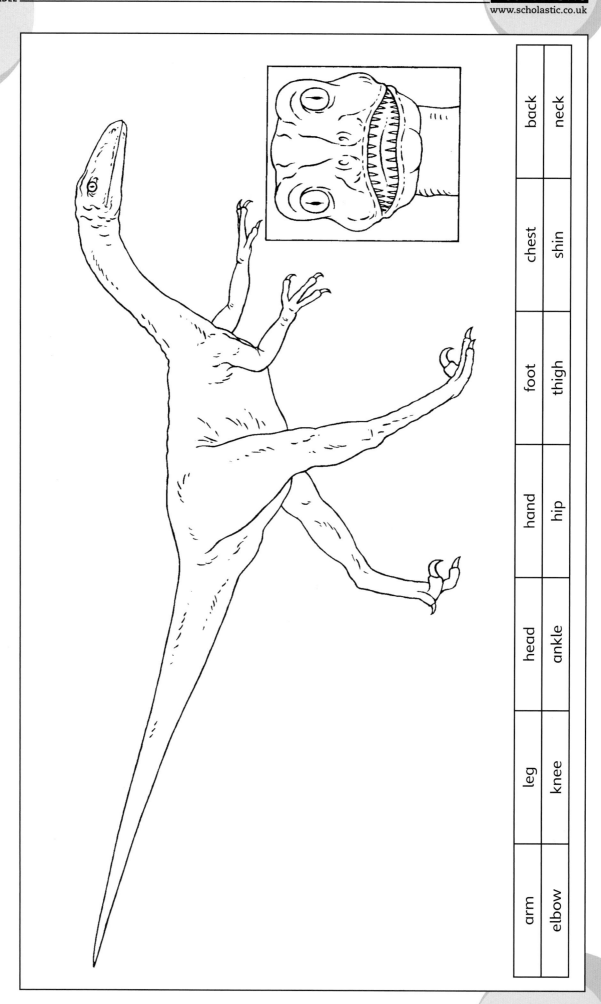

arm	leg	head	hand	foot	chest	back
elbow	knee	ankle	hip	thigh	shin	neck

HOT TOPICS Dinosaurs

Theme 3 Neck and tails

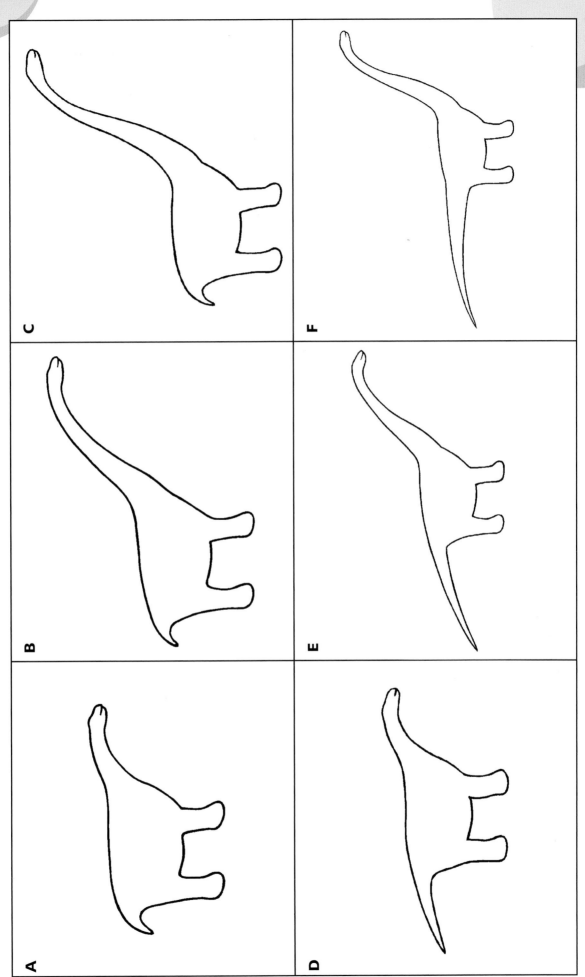

A

B

C

D

E

F

SCHOLASTIC
www.scholastic.co.uk

Theme 3 Dinosaur leg bones

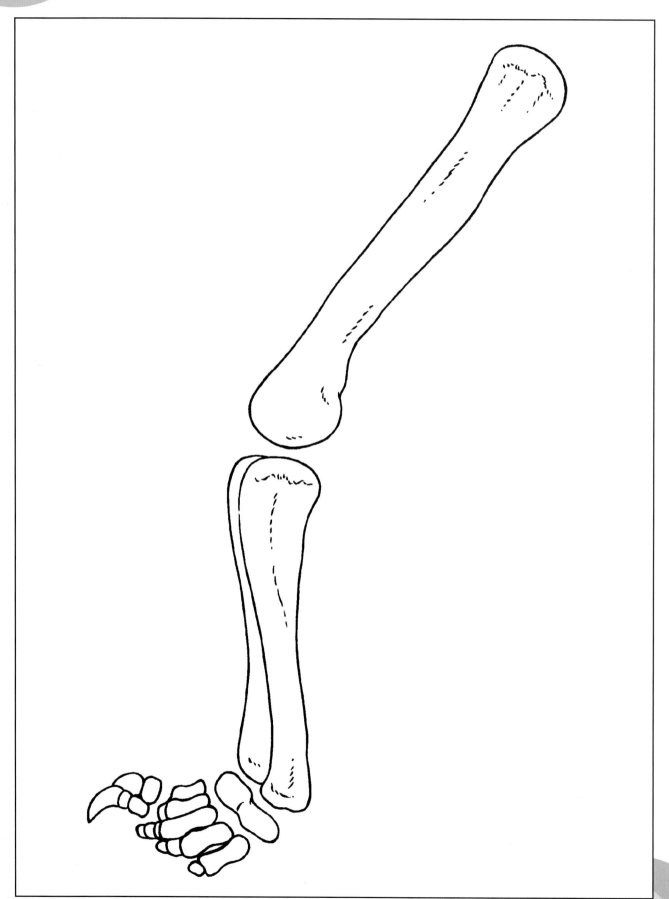

Dinosaurs on the move

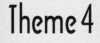

BACKGROUND

Many dinosaurs left footprints behind. A group of dinosaur footprints is called a 'trackway'. This formed when a dinosaur moved over soft mud, perhaps alongside a river or across a drying lake bed. In time, the mud set to stone and the depressions left by the feet were preserved. Large plant-eating dinosaurs like Apatosaurus had feet similar to, but larger than, those of an elephant. They left large, rounded footprints of a 'wash tub' shape. Some prints are so large that if one was filled with water, a child could have a bath in it! Predatory dinosaurs, such as Tyrannosaurus, had three-toed feet and left footprints that look a bit like arrows. The arrows point to where the dinosaur had been, not where it was going.

Palaeontologists can use dinosaur footprints and trackways to:
- estimate a dinosaur's mass by measuring the depth of the footprints
- discover whether the dinosaur walked flat-footed or on tiptoe
- estimate the size of the dinosaur by relating its stride to its hip height
- calculate the speed of the dinosaur from its foot size, hip height and stride length.

THE CONTENTS

Lesson 1 (Ages 5–7)
Dinosaur feet and tracks
The children compare their own feet with a dinosaur's foot. They make a footprint and compare a flat foot with one on tiptoe. They make a dinosaur trackway using model dinosaur feet.

Lesson 2 (Ages 7–9)
Dinosaur strides and tracks
The children look at some dinosaur trackways and try to interpret them. They try to find out which is the largest and test the idea that the length of the stride relates to leg length and hip height.

Lesson 3 (Ages 9–11)
Dinosaur tracks and speed
The children examine a trackway and discover that dinosaurs varied their stride. They use this to interpret their behaviour by measuring how stride length is related to speed.

Notes on photocopiables

Three trackways (page 36)
This sheet shows an imaginary trackway of a large animal (A), accompanied by a smaller animal of the same species (B). A second species (C), similar in size to A, has also left tracks. It is not possible to say whether C went by before or after the other two, but they did not collide.

Stride length and hip height (page 37)
This compares the stride length and hip height of a dinosaur and a person. To help the children focus, it contains a table for them to fill in which can be converted into a spreadsheet for ICT work.

Two trackways (page 38)
This shows an imaginary trackway of two dinosaurs. Dinosaur A is a herbivore which plods along, stops, and then moves more quickly. B is a predator which is moving very slowly, then sprints at A and runs behind it, moving in to attack from the other side.

PHOTOGRAPH © NATURAL HISTORY MUSEUM

Lesson 1 Dinosaur feet and tracks

AGES 5–7

Objectives
● To compare human feet with dinosaur feet.
● To make a model dinosaur trackway.
● To make simple inferences from footprints and trackways.

Subject references
Science
● Use first hand experience and simple information sources to answer questions. (NC: KS1 Sc1 2b)
● Make simple comparisons and identify simple patterns and associations. (NC: KS1 Sc1 2h)
Art and design
● Try out techniques and apply these to materials and processes. (NC: KS1 2b)

Resources and preparation
● Set up on the floor a deep tray filled with sand.
● Make dinosaur feet by twisting three pipe cleaners together and splaying the wires at one end to make a three-toed foot, or make feet using one pipe cleaner as shown in the pictures below. Each child will need a pair of pipe-cleaner feet so that they can simulate walking. (With older children, give them the pipe cleaners to make their own feet.)
● Provide paint samples in several colours in small shallow trays, saucers or bowls.
● Provide plenty of plain A4 paper.
● Find pictures of dinosaur tracks in reference books.
● This lesson can be adapted to be part of your Dinosaur Day.

What to do
● Show the children the reference books and ask them to look at the different tracks and shapes of dinosaur feet.
● Encourage the children to think about how they could make visual comparisons between the dinosaur tracks and their own footprints. Lead them towards the idea of putting a foot in sand, and let one or more of them make footprints in the tray of sand.

Look at the footprints and compare the shape with the dinosaur footprints in the reference books.
● Tell the children that a group of dinosaur footprints is called a 'trackway'. Explain that they are going to make a trackway using dinosaur feet made from pipe cleaners.
● Demonstrate to the class how to pick up paint with the pipe-cleaner feet and place them down to make footprints. Then let the children make their own trackways on clean sheets of paper.
● As the children begin creating their trackways, talk about strides, and show the children that footprints are far apart when a long stride is made, and near together when a short stride is made.

Extension
● Encourage more confident learners to make footprints showing the difference between standing on flat feet and standing on tiptoe. Explain that some small dinosaurs such as Fabrosaurus ran on tiptoe. Ask the children to mime being this dinosaur.
● Alternatively, the children could make drawings of dinosaur feet on paper, cut them out and place them across the classroom to make a giant trackway.

PHOTOGRAPGH © PETER ROWE

HOT TOPICS Dinosaurs

Lesson 2 Dinosaur strides and tracks

Resources and preparation
● Make copies of page 36, 'Three trackways', and page 37, 'Stride length and hip height', for each child.
● Have an enlarged copy of page 13, 'Four dinosaurs', available for reference.
● Collect six to eight round washing-up bowls of the same size.
● Each group will need standard rulers and metre rules.

Starter
● Bring the washing-up bowls into the classroom and lay them out across the room as dinosaur footprints. Tell the children that these bowls represent the footprints of a very large dinosaur. Explain that large footprints that are this shape are known as 'wash tub' prints and they are made by dinosaurs such as Apatosaurus. Remind the children what Apatosaurus looked like and encourage them to imagine it walking and making these footprints.
● Invite the children to compare the size and shape of their feet with the bowls. Encourage a child to step inside one of the bowls to demonstrate the difference in size.

What to do
● Show the children the 'Three trackways' photocopiable sheet and ask them to say what they think the combination of trackways tells us. Can they arrange animals A, B and C in order of size? They should agree that animal B is the smallest, but the children may disagree about animals A and C.
● Encourage the children to think of another way to compare sizes of animals from the information in their prints. Interpreting trackways of dinosaurs that walk on four legs is complex so ask the children to imagine a large and small dinosaur (like yourself and one of the children) that walks on two legs. Walk about and encourage the child to do the same. Ask the children how the way the large and small dinosaur walk may be related to the size. Look for an answer about the length of the stride (the length of one step). Can they think of a way to find out if the length of the stride is related to the size of the animal making it?
● Discuss the children's oral or written responses and then give out the 'Stride

length and hip height' photocopiable sheet. Ask them to carry out an investigation to see how correct their ideas are regarding animal size and stride length. Show them how to measure and how to fill in their data on the sheet.

● Point out that, in this investigation, a measure of body size is hip height as this is what palaeontologists use. Let the children carry out their investigations, if possible enlisting the help of adults or other children.

Differentiation

● Encourage less confident learners to measure their own stride and each other's hip heights, or the stride and hip height of an adult helper.

● Ask more confident learners to measure the full length of three strides and find an average stride length to use in their data.

Assessment

The children can be assessed on whether they decide to arrange individuals in order of hip height and look at the stride lengths, or whether they need help with this. They can also be assessed on the way they

describe the link between stride length and hip height.

Plenary

Conclude the investigation by saying that stride length is a measure of body size because people with higher hip heights make longer strides than people with lower hip heights. Ask the children to look back at the 'Three trackways' photocopiable sheet and to measure the stride lengths of dinosaurs A and C. They should find that dinosaur A makes slightly longer strides than C and is therefore probably larger.

Outcomes

● The children can take measurements.

● The children can arrange the measurements and look for relationships.

● The children can conclude that larger animals make longer strides than smaller animals.

PHOTOGRAPH © PETER ROWE

Lesson 3 Dinosaur tracks and speed

PHOTOGRAPH © QAMAR, STOCK.XCHNG

Objectives
• To interpret information revealed by a trackway.
• To take measurements.
• To use data from measurements to interpret a trackway.

Subject references
Science
• Ask questions that can be investigated scientifically and decide how to find answers. (NC: KS2 Sc1 2a)
• Make systematic measurements. (NC: KS2 Sc1 2f)
• Identify a simple pattern. (NC: KS2 Sc1 2i)
Mathematics
• Recognise need for standard units of length. (NC: KS2 Ma3 4a)
• Read scales with increasing accuracy. (NC: KS2 Ma3 4b)
• Use data-handling skills. (NC: KS2 Ma4 1a)
ICT
• Investigate the effect of changing values and identifying patterns and relationships. (NC: KS2 2c)
English
• Create different roles. (NC: KS2 En1 4a)
• Imagine ideas. (NC: KS2 En3 9a)
• Inform and explain. (NC: KS2 En3 9b)

Resources and preparation
• Make copies of page 38, 'Two trackways' for each group and an enlarged or OHT version for class use.
• Provide standard rulers and metre rules for each group.
• Make internet access and/or dinosaur reference books available.
• This lesson can be adapted to be part of your Dinosaur Day.

What to do
• Show the children the 'Two trackways' photocopiable sheet and ask them what they think the tracks of footprints show. Elicit that each animal seems to change not only the direction but the size of its stride. What, do the children think, could the animals be doing? Look for an answer about speeding up and slowing down.
• Ask the children to devise a way of testing out the hypothesis that the speed at which something moves affects its stride. Suggest they measure the stride of someone strolling along and then someone walking quickly. They should find that as someone moves faster their stride increases.

Help the children to relate the findings of their investigation to the incident shown by the footprints on the photocopiable sheet.
• Tell the children that palaeontologists use foot size, hip height and stride length in calculations to work out how fast dinosaurs could move. Challenge the children to use the internet or information books to find the speeds at which different-sized dinosaurs could move.

Extension
• Encourage the children to interpret the event shown by the trackways as described in Notes on photocopiables on page 31. They could then either write a story about what happened next or explain what the trackways show.
• Ask the children to consider what a limping trackway would look like for an animal walking on two legs, if (for example), dinosaur B bit dinosaur A and made it limp? Explain that one stride will be shorter than the other.

TOPICS Dinosaurs

Theme 4 Three trackways

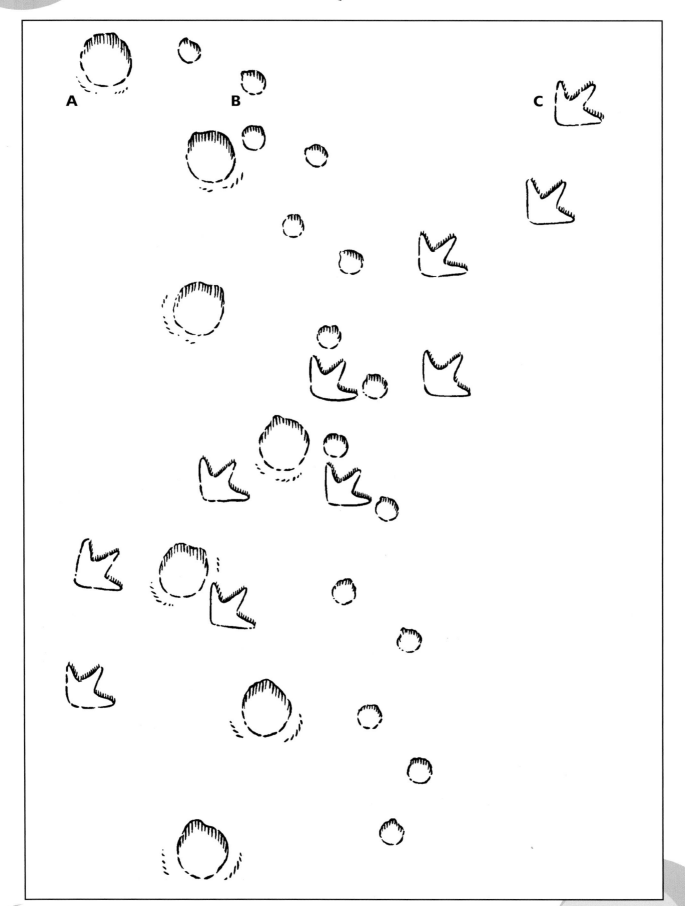

Theme 4 Stride length and hip height

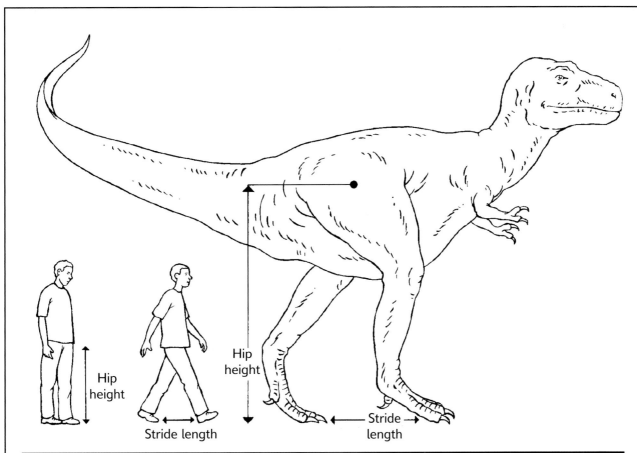

Hip
height

Hip
height

Hip
height

Stride length

Stride
length

Stride
length

Person's name	Hip height (cm)	Stride length (cm)

Theme 4 Two trackways

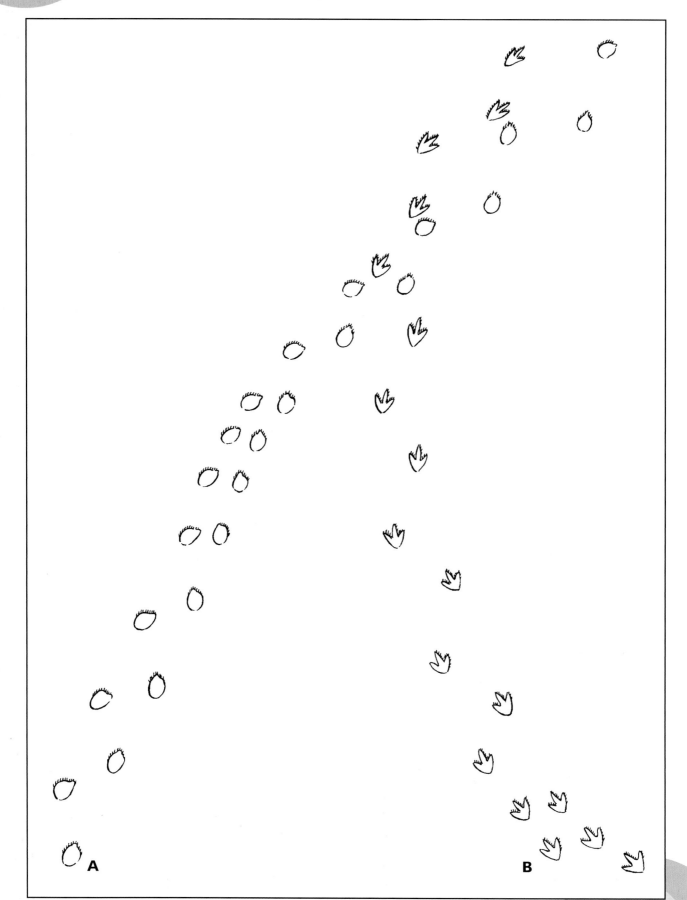

Dinosaur food

BACKGROUND

Some children may think that all dinosaurs were ferocious but this is not true. Many fed on plants and would reserve any ferociousness for defence against predators.

Large plant-eating dinosaurs with long necks did not have cheeks in which to store food so that it could be chewed. They had peg-like teeth that raked through leaves and pulled them off branches. The plant material was then churned up in the stomach with stones that the dinosaur had also swallowed. About 40 stones were found with one dinosaur skeleton. Later herbivorous dinosaurs, such as Tenontosaurus, had cheeks in which to store food and wide teeth at the back of the jaw to grind up food.

Carnivores had pointed teeth, which could penetrate flesh easily and grip prey. Their teeth were designed to bring the prey to a quick death, as lengthy fighting could result in the predator being wounded. Carcharodontosaurus had teeth with serrated edges, like sharks'.

The dung of some dinosaurs has fossilised. Pieces of fossilised dinosaur dung are called 'coprolites'. One of the largest pieces found measures about 44 by 16 by 13cm, and is thought to have been produced by a Tyrannosaurus. Coprolites from herbivores contain pieces of wood, leaves and seeds, while carnivores produced coprolites containing bone, shells, teeth and fish scales.

THE CONTENTS

Lesson 1 (Ages 5–7)
Teeth and biting
The children compare the teeth of dinosaurs and make models to see which one makes the deeper bite. They discover that teeth with serrated edges are better cutters.

Lesson 2 (Ages 7–9)
Grinding up food
The children discover that some dinosaurs had stones in their stomachs to help them grind up food. They investigate the effect of stones on plant material.

Lesson 3 (Ages 9–11)
Dinosaur food chains
The children construct food chains and trace the path of food through a food web.

Notes on photocopiables

Dinosaur teeth (page 44)
Allosaurus used its teeth for stabbing. Tenontosaurus used its teeth for grinding up plant material. The two dinosaur skulls represent a carnivore and a herbivore. The model teeth should be approximately five centimetres long and just over one centimetre at their widest point. The markings on the match should be roughly three millimetres apart.

Grinding up food (page 45)
The two beakers show the fair test and there are spaces for the children to make drawings of their observations.

A dinosaur food web (page 46)
There are only a few instances where a dinosaur skeleton has been found with the skeleton of another dinosaur inside it. However, some generalisations using dinosaur groups can be made to construct a food web. The groups are: tyrannosaurids; dromaeosaurids (eg Velociraptor); ornithomimids (eg Gallimimus); pachycephalosaurs; ankylosaurs; hadrosaurs; ceratopsians (eg Triceratops).

These dinosaurs can also be split into three groups of:
herbivores (Triceratops, Hadrosaurus, Pachycephalosaurus and Ankylosaurus); carnivores (Tyrannosaurus and Velociraptor); omnivores (Gallimimus).

PHOTOGRAPH © SASAN, STOCK.XCHNG

Lesson 1 Teeth and biting

Objective
● To compare dinosaur teeth by performing experiments using models.

Subject references
Science
● Making observations and measurements.
(NC: KS1 Sc1 1)
● Recognise when a test is unfair.
(NC: KS1 Sc1 2d)

Resources and preparation
● Make a copy of page 44, 'Dinosaur teeth', for each child.
● Each group will need a cup or small bowl, some plain flour, a spoon and a ruler.
● The children will also need Plasticine, a spent long matchstick and a ballpoint pen (to put marks on the matchstick).
● Have serrated and smooth plastic knives for demonstration (for the Extension).

What to do
● Point out to the children the two pictures of the dinosaur skulls on the photocopiable sheet. Invite them to look carefully at the teeth in each skull and decide which one would give the deepest bite and help a predator to wound and catch its prey. Encourage the children to explain their answers by referring to the shape, size, number and position of the teeth.
● Now tell the children that scientists sometimes make models when they want to test an idea. Show them a piece of Plasticine and explain that they are going to make their own models of a pointed tooth and a flat tooth, using the diagrams on the photocopiable sheet to help them.
● Spoon flour into the cup and smooth off its surface. Tell the children that this represents the side of a dinosaur's body.
● Remind the class how to make a fair test and let them drop each tooth from the same height (approximately ten centimetres is best) into the flour. The children may find that sometimes the tooth falls sideways, so remind them that experiments must be tried a few times to ensure fair and genuine results.

● When each tooth has made a hole, let the children judge by eye which one is the deepest. Ask them to think about how they could make a small measuring device to put in the hole.
● After they have made a few suggestions, produce the long matchstick. Show the class how to put regular markings on the stick and insert it carefully into the hole to compare depths. Were their eye-judgements correct? Was the result what they expected?

Extension
● Carefully show the children a plastic knife with a smooth edge and a plastic knife with a serrated edge. Explain that some dinosaurs had teeth with smooth sides and others had teeth with tiny 'saw teeth' on them. Ask the children to guess which would be better for cutting with.
● Give them a flat piece of Plasticine and show them how to carefully test how easy or difficult it is to cut through the Plasticine with each knife.

Did you know?
Amygdalodon had spoon-shaped teeth and Edmontosaurus had teeth shaped like diamonds.

Lesson 2 Grinding up food

Resources and preparation

- Make a copy of 'Grinding up food' on page 45 for each child.
- Find a length of coniferous twig with leaves, for example, leylandii or fir.

Safety note: Do not use yew as it is poisonous.

- You will also need a comb and a stopwatch or kitchen timer.
- Each group will need a shallow tray and two plastic beakers with screw-top lids. One beaker from each pair must contain eight pebbles varying in size from 2 to 4cm long.
- Each group will also need six pieces of lettuce about 6 to 8cm square.
- For the Extension, insert seeds, pips or bits of leaf into pieces of Plasticine, and have a plastic knife available. (Do not use nuts when talking about seeds and pips.)
- This lesson can be adapted to be part of your Dinosaur Day.

Starter

- Give the children a copy of the photocopiable sheet and tell them that the dinosaur Diplodocus had teeth that were like pegs, with gaps between them like the teeth of a comb. Take the coniferous twig and 'comb' it so that some leaves come off. Reposition the twig in the comb if the leaves fail to come off at first.
- Tell the children that this is how the large dinosaurs like Diplodocus gathered leaves from trees. Continue to explain that the dinosaurs did not have cheeks in which to place their food, which meant they could not chew it. Therefore, they had to swallow their food whole.

What to do

- Tell the children that some dinosaurs' skeletons have been found with groups of stones in the place where their stomachs would have been. Palaeontologists think that the dinosaurs swallowed the stones to help them to break up and digest their food, as some birds still do today.

Safety note: Ensure that you stress to the children that they should never swallow stones, however small, as this is very dangerous.

- Tell the children that they are going to test how effective a dinosaur's stomach full of stones is at grinding up food, compared to a stomach without stones.
- Explain that the plastic beakers are going to be their model dinosaur stomachs. Then, give the children three pieces of lettuce for each 'stomach' and let them draw a picture on their sheet of what the lettuce leaves look like before they are put into the plastic beaker 'stomachs'.
- Describe how the muscles in the dinosaur stomach wall would slowly churn up the food. In this experiment they are going to shake the stomachs to represent this digestion process at high speed. Ask the class to feed three pieces of lettuce into each 'stomach' and make sure that they screw the lids on securely.
- Invite the children to write down their predictions about what the food will look like after the stomachs have been shaken. *Will the lettuce leaves in the stomach full of stones look different from the lettuce leaves in the stomach that does not include stones? How will they differ? Why do the children think this?* They should make the distinction in their written prediction on the sheet.
- Tell the group to shake their 'stomachs' for two minutes, making sure that you time them using the stopwatch. Then invite the children to open the beakers and tip out the contents into the trays.

AGES 7–9

Objective
- To carry out an investigation on 'stomach stones'.

Subject references
Science
- Make a fair test.
(NC: KS2 Sc1 2d)
- Use drawings to communicate data.
(NC: KS2 Sc1 2h)

- Ask the children to draw what the stomach contents look like on their photocopiable sheet and to compare the results with their predictions. *What was the difference between the lettuce leaves in the stomach full of stones and the lettuce leaves in the empty stomach? Why was this?*

Differentiation

- Some children may need to work with an adult helper while conducting the experiment and in wording their predictions.
- Extend children by asking them to repeat the experiment and compare the two sets of results.

Assessment

Assess the children on the quality of their drawings as representing what they saw, the prediction they made and how they compared the result with their prediction.

Plenary

- Ask each group to report their findings to the class. Has everyone come to the same conclusion?
- The lesson can be extended by telling the children that fossilised dinosaur dung has been discovered and when scientists have examined it, they have found out what the dinosaur had been eating. Give each group a piece of model dinosaur dung made from a Plasticine in which you have placed a piece of leaf, seeds or pips. Encourage the children to use a plastic knife to cut it open carefully and discover what the dinosaur had eaten.

Outcomes

- The children can record their observations as drawings.
- They can make a prediction and test this prediction with a fair test.

PHOTOGRAPH © PETER ROWE

Lesson 3 Dinosaur food chains

PHOTOGRAPH © MMAGALLAN, STOCK.XCHNG

AGES 9–11

Objectives
● To build up food chains from information provided.
● To understand the relationship between food chains and food webs.

Subject references
Science
● Use food chains to show feeding relationships in a habitat. (NC: KS2 Sc2 5d)
● Show nearly all food chains start with green plants. (NC: KS2 Sc2 5e)

Resources and preparation
● Make copies of page 46, 'A dinosaur food web'.
● Ensure the children have coloured pencils or highlighter pens.

What to do
● Tell the children that dinosaurs lived in particular habitats just as animals do today. There were food chains in the habitats to which the dinosaurs belonged. Ask the children to construct, on paper, food chains from the following information:
  ● Triceratops fed on plants and Tyrannosaurus fed on Triceratops.
    (Plants > Triceratops > Tyrannosaurus)
  ● Ankylosaurus fed on plants, Velociraptor fed on Ankylosaurus and Tyrannosaurus fed on Velociraptor.
    (Plants > Ankylosaurus > Velociraptor > Tyrannosaurus)
  ● Insects fed on plants, Gallimimus fed on insects, Velociraptor fed on Gallimimus and Tyrannosaurus fed on Velociraptor.
    (Plants > Insects > Gallimimus > Velociraptor >Tyrannosaurus)
● Explain to the children that food chains can be linked together to form food webs.

Give out copies of the photocopiable sheet and ask the children to colour in on the food web the food chains that they have made.
● Ask the class to describe the diet of Hadrosaurus and Gallimimus. Can the children explain how Tyrannosaurus' diet was different from Velociraptor's? (It included Velociraptor.)
● Challenge the children to identify which dinosaurs were herbivores, which were carnivores and which one was an omnivore.

Extension
Invite the children to think about questions, such as the following examples, to develop their knowledge of how different factors can affect a habitat and everything that lives in it:
  ● *What would Gallimimus have to do if the lizards disappeared from the habitat?* (Eat more plants and insects.)
  ● *What would Velociraptor have to do if Triceratops and Hadrosaurus disappeared from the habitat?* (Eat more Pachycephalosauruses, Ankylosauruses and Gallimimuses.)
  ● *What would happen if all the plants died out?* (All the dinosaurs, insects and lizards would die too.)

PHOTOGRAPH © PETER ROWE,
MODELS © WWW.EVERYTHINGDINOSAUR.COM

Theme 5 Dinosaur teeth

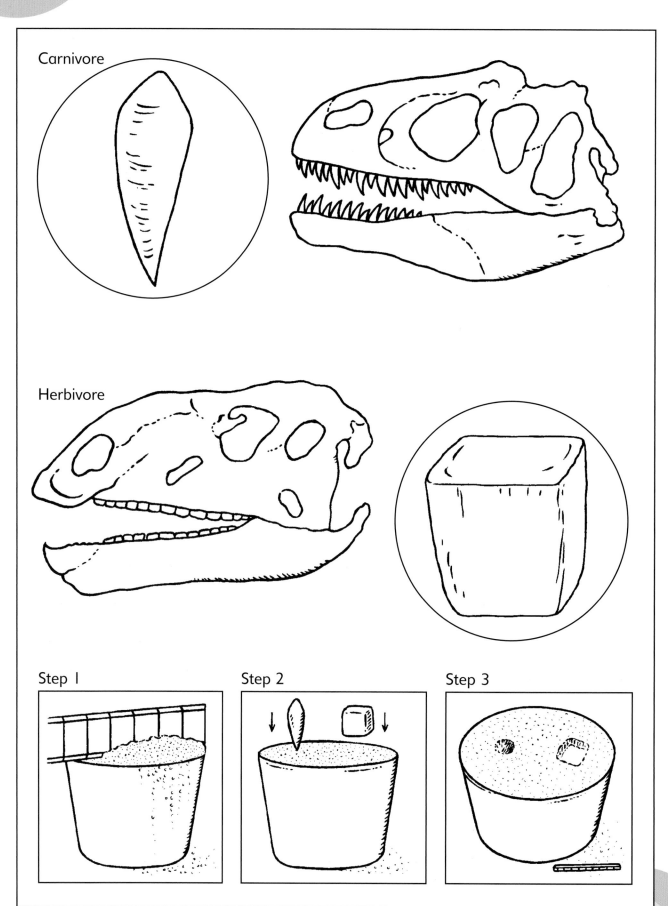

Carnivore

Herbivore

Step 1

Step 2

Step 3

Theme 5 Grinding up food

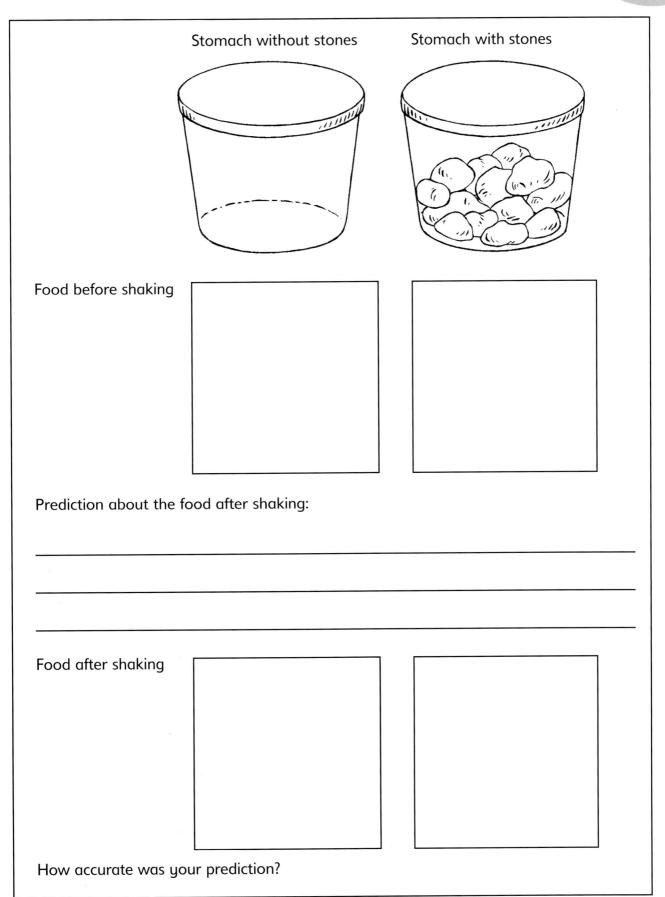

Stomach without stones   Stomach with stones

Food before shaking

Prediction about the food after shaking:

_____

_____

_____

Food after shaking

How accurate was your prediction?

Theme 5 A dinosaur food web

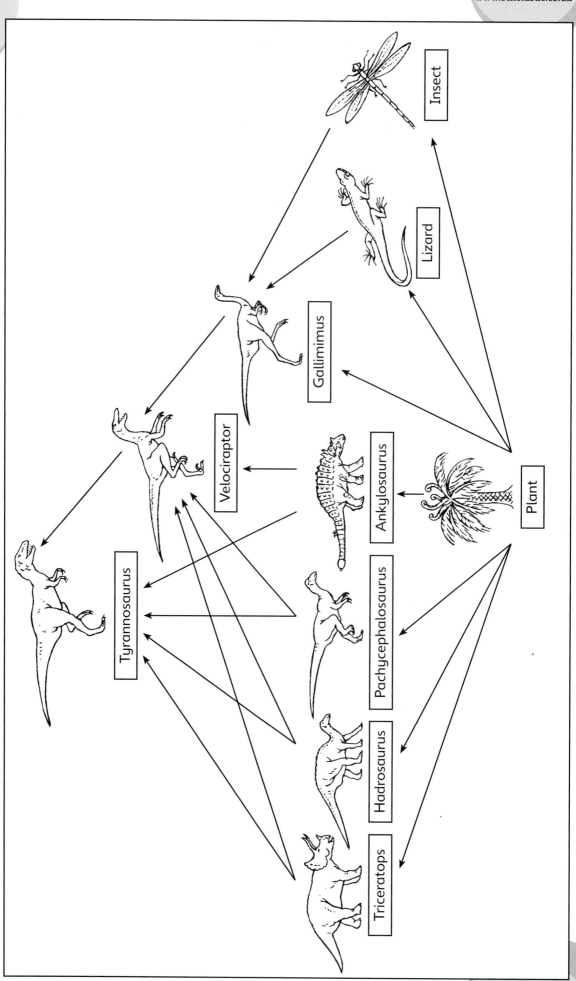

Insect

Lizard

Gallimimus

Velociraptor

Ankylosaurus

Plant

Tyrannosaurus

Pachycephalosaurus

Hadrosaurus

Triceratops

Attack and defence

BACKGROUND

Carnivorous dinosaurs attacked their prey in a range of ways. They had sharp pointed teeth with which they could stab and hold their prey. Some dinosaurs, such as Velociraptor, had sharp claws on their hind feet which slashed at prey as they jumped on it.

It is thought that some dinosaurs hunted alone and crept up on their prey to take them by surprise. Some small dinosaurs, such as Velociraptor, hunted in packs to bring down a large dinosaur.

Herbivorous dinosaurs had various methods of defence. Some, such as Apatosaurus, grew so big that no other dinosaur, or group of dinosaurs, could bring down an adult if it remained healthy. Other dinosaurs, like Gallimimus, could run quickly away if attacked.

Many dinosaurs were too large and heavy to run away, but had protective 'armour'. Nodosaurus had armour along its back, Stegosaurus had bony plates, and Triceratops had a huge head shield. It also had horns and could charge at predators. Ankylosaurus had pointed armour on its back and a large club on its tail, which it swung at attackers. It could knock over and possibly break the legs of some dinosaurs. The club was about 119cm long, 66cm wide and 13cm thick.

Dinosaurs, like other living things, adapted to their environment. Many scientists believe that such defence tools developed over generations. In a similar way, predators developed better means of attack in response to the herbivores' improved defences.

Lesson 1 (Ages 5–7)
Dinosaur clubs
The children test the idea that a larger club will give an attacker a more powerful knock than a small club.

Lesson 2 (Ages 7–9)
Into attack
The children make a dinosaur head which opens its mouth and makes a sound.

Lesson 3 (Ages 9–11)
Attacking a dinosaur herd
The children play a simple game to see how some dinosaur species adapted to their predators' attacks.

Notes on photocopiables
Dinosaur clubs (page 52)
A model club, made from string and Plasticine, is shown ready to be released at a model dinosaur on the end of a ruler. A table is provided for the children to record data.

Attacking heads (page 53)
Two arrangements are shown for making a dinosaur head that moves by pneumatics and makes a sound using electricity. The first model is the easiest to make.

Dinosaur head and jaws (page 54)
These templates can be photocopied onto grey-green card for the children to cut out and assemble to make dinosaur jaws.

Attacking a dinosaur herd (page 55)
The children play a game to show how a group of dinosaurs can survive being attacked.

PHOTOGRAPH © OMSTER-COM, STOCK.XCHNG

Lesson 1 Dinosaur clubs

AGES 5–7

Objective
● To investigate how the size of a club on a model tail affects the size of its push.

Subject references
Science
● Think about what might happen before deciding what to do.
(NC: KS1 Sc1 2c)
● Recognise when a test is unfair.
(NC: KS1 Sc1 2d)
● Follow simple instructions to control the risks to themselves and others.
(NC: KS1 Sc1 2e)
● Know that pushes and pulls are examples of forces.
(NC: KS1 Sc4 2b)

Resources and preparation
● Photocopy page 52, 'Dinosaur clubs', for each child.
● Prepare lumps of Plasticine 1cm, 2cm and 3cm across, for each child or group.
● You will need pieces of string 15cm long, small model dinosaurs, rulers or half-metre rules and a range of masses from 0.5kg to 2kg (these could be small bags of flour).
● Provide pictures of Ankylosaurus in reference books.

What to do
● Ask the children to look at pictures of Ankylosaurus. Point out the bony armour along the back and sides and then examine the club at the end of the tail. Do the children think the size of the club affects its capability to knock over or wound its attackers? Can they suggest an experiment to test this idea?
● Remind the children that when scientists carry out experiments they often use models. In this experiment they are going to use a model Ankylosaurus tail, which swings down rather than across. Show them the diagram of the experiment set-up on the photocopiable sheet.

● Help the children to arrange the experiment as shown and to carry out their tests, writing down the results in the table provided. They should find that the larger the club, the further it knocks the model dinosaur.
● Ask the children why Ankylosaurus did not have a larger club. Help them to understand that as a club gets larger it also gets heavier, and let the children hold the different masses of flour. They should come to the conclusion that a very large club would be too heavy to swing, so the ideal club is one heavy enough to be effective but light enough to swing and manoeuvre.

Extension
● If you have a model Stegosaurus, ask the children to look at its tail to see that it does not have a club, but has a bunch of spines. Ask: *how will the spines help to protect the dinosaur?* Look for an answer about stabbing the attacker.
● If the children have not yet completed Theme 5 Lesson 1 'Teeth and biting' (page 40), adapt that lesson to test the idea that sharp spines stab deeper than blunt spines.

ILLUSTRATION © LASZLO VERES/BEEHIVE ILLUSTRATION

Lesson 2 Into attack

Resources and preparation
- Photocopy page 53, 'Attacking heads', for each child.
- Photocopy 'Dinosaur head and jaws', page 54, onto green card for each group.
- Provide sticky tape, paper and scissors for each group.
- Also provide a balloon and straw or two syringes connected by a plastic tube.
- Each group will also need a cell, three wires, a buzzer and a switch.

Starter
- Ask the children if they have ever been to a museum and seen model dinosaurs that move. Explain that the models move by having simple machinery in which air or a liquid is squeezed. (Many museum models are powered by electricity and use air (pneumatics) or a liquid (hydraulics) to make pistons move.)
- Explain to the children that they are going to make their own dinosaur models in which air is squeezed so that the model moves. Tell them that the models will also use electricity to make a sound.
- Tell the children that you want them to make a dinosaur head that is about to attack. It should open its mouth so its teeth are ready to stab and it should also make a noise to frighten its prey. Such a noise might make the prey stop moving for a moment and make it easier to attack.

What to do
- Show the children the 'Attacking heads' photocopiable sheet and indicate that, in the first diagram, the mouth is opened by a balloon inside it being inflated, and the buzzer is attached to the back of the head outside the mouth.
- In the second version, the mouth is opened by forcing the air in syringe A into syringe B, which pushes up the top part of the jaw, and the buzzer is installed inside the head, towards the front of the mouth.
- If there is sufficient equipment and materials, and it is appropriate, let the children decide which model they would like to make. Alternatively, you could set different heads to different groups, or they could all make the same head.
- Now give the children the green card which has the 'Dinosaur head and jaws' templates photocopied on to them. Help the children to cut out and assemble the upper and lower jaw.
- Show the children how to join the two jaws together by making a paper hinge and sticking it to the back of the upper and lower jaw.
- Demonstrate how to pierce a hole in the paper hinge for the straw or tube to fit through (depending on which model is made).
- If the children are making the heads with the syringes, they will need to devise a way

AGES 7–9

Objectives
- To make a model dinosaur head which uses air to produce movement.
- To make a model dinosaur head which uses electricity to produce sounds.
- This lesson can be adapted to be part of your Dinosaur Day.

Subject references
Design and technology
- Generate ideas for products.
(NC: KS2 1a)
- Plan what they have to do.
(NC: KS2 1c)
- Select appropriate tools and techniques for making their product.
(NC: KS2 2a)
- Recognise that the quality of the product depends on how well it is made and how well it meets its intended purpose.
(NC: KS2 3c)
Science
- Construct circuits to make electrical devices work.
(NC: KS2 Sc4 1a)

of securing the syringe to the inside of the top and bottom jaw.

- Show the children how to assemble the simple circuit which includes the buzzer.
- Finally, the groups need to work out a way of making the buzzer sound and the mouth open at the same time so that the dinosaur roars (by simultaneously inflating the balloon or syringe and pressing the switch in the circuit).

Differentiation

- To support less confident learners, the head and jaws can be made up before the lesson so that the children can concentrate on working with adult helpers to install the movement- and sound-making equipment.
- Encourage more confident learners to make a dinosaur head from a selection of boxes. They may like to add eyes on top of the head and paper cones for teeth.

Assessment

The children can be assessed on the way they plan their work and carry it out by working together. They can also be assessed on the quality of the hinge and organisation of the circuit. If they have used the syringes, assess them on how well the mouth can be opened and closed several times.

Plenary

Ask the children to show their attacking dinosaurs in turn. Demonstrate each one a few times to test for signs of wear.

Outcomes

- The children can use materials and equipment safely.
- They can make a working model which uses air for movement and electricity for sound.

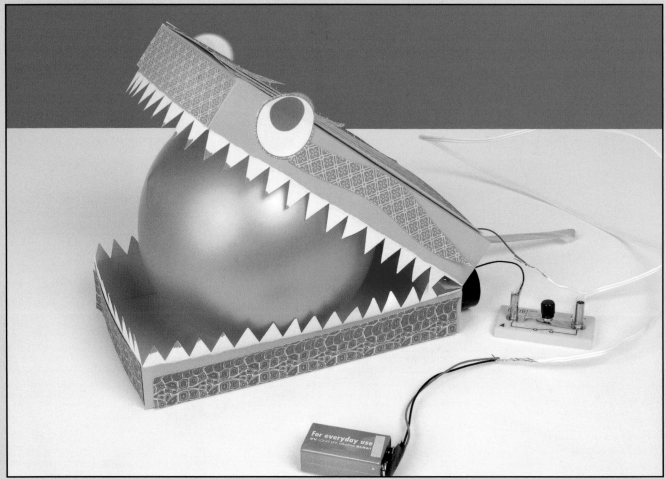

PHOTOGRAPH © PETER ROWE

Lesson 3 Attacking a dinosaur herd

Resources and preparation
● Make a card copy of page 55, 'Attacking a dinosaur herd', for each group.
● Provide each group with a dice, scissors and a stopwatch.

What to do
● Tell the children that they are going to see how the attacks of a predator can make a species adapt to its surroundings.
● Ask the children to cut out the game board and the dinosaur counters at the bottom of the sheet. Tell them to put the predator on one of the corner squares and to spread out the other dinosaurs randomly in squares all over the board.
● The game is played in the following way: Roll the dice and move the predator that number of moves in any direction over the board. If it lands on a square with a dinosaur without horns, it eats it straight away and removes it from the board. If it lands on a dinosaur with horns, you must roll the dice again and only remove the dinosaur if you roll an even number. If you roll an odd number, the dinosaur with horns stays on the board and you must roll the dice again to move the predator on. This shows that dinosaurs with horns are more difficult to kill.
● The children should set the stopwatch and try to eat as many dinosaurs in the herd as possible in two minutes. At the end of that time, ask them to count up the number of dinosaurs with and without horns remaining.

● Allow the children to play the game three times. It should be found that the herd has more dinosaurs with horns in it after each attack.
● Tell the children that as more dinosaurs with horns survive, there is a good chance that they will also produce dinosaurs with horns when they breed so that, in time, the whole herd would comprise of dinosaurs with horns. This makes it more difficult for predators to attack them.

Extension
● Encourage the children to speculate on how a predator can become adapted to a herd of dinosaurs with horns on their heads, so that it increases its chance of getting a meal. Prompt them to consider the ability to move in quickly and attack the rear of the herd of prey dinosaurs.
● Then speculate on how the horned dinosaurs can adapt to survive a dinosaur that always attacks from the rear. Look for an answer about dinosaurs developing spikes down their back to survive longer.

Did you know?
Pachycephalosaurus had a head shaped like a crash helmet, which it used to butt other dinosaurs.

PHOTOGRAPH © PETER ROWE

HOTTOPICS Dinosaurs

Theme 6 Dinosaur clubs

How to set up the experiment

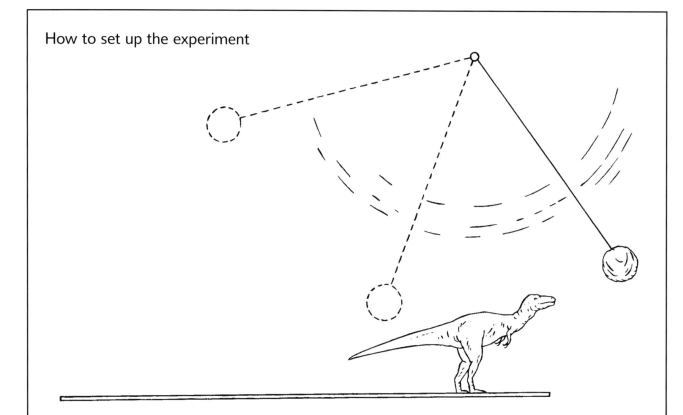

Model club size	Attempt 1 (cm)	Attempt 2 (cm)	Attempt 3 (cm)
1cm			
2cm			
3cm			

Theme 6 Attacking heads

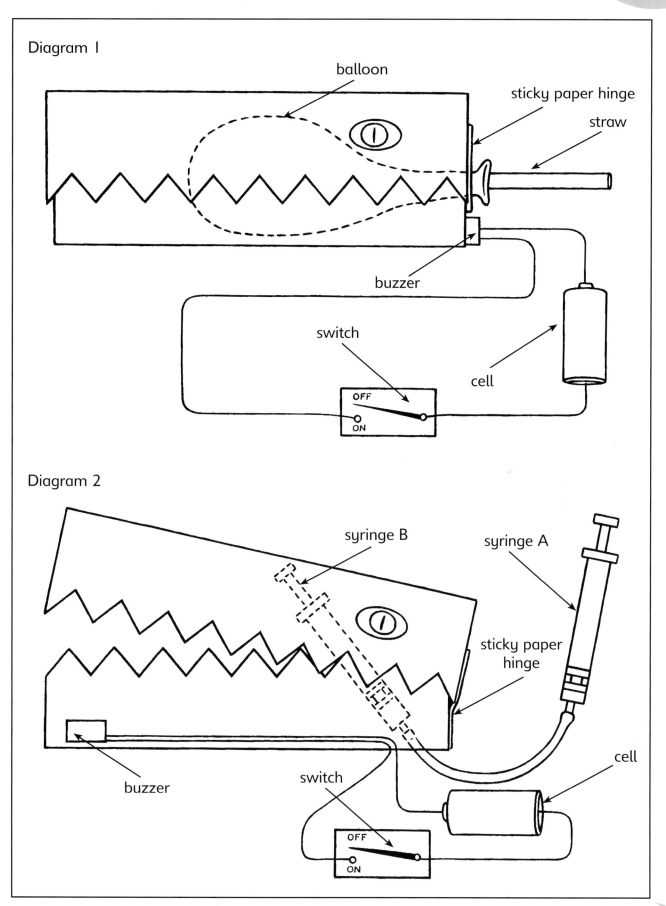

Diagram 1

balloon

sticky paper hinge

straw

buzzer

switch

cell

Diagram 2

syringe B

syringe A

sticky paper hinge

buzzer

switch

cell

SCHOLASTIC
www.scholastic.co.uk

Theme 6 Dinosaur head and jaws

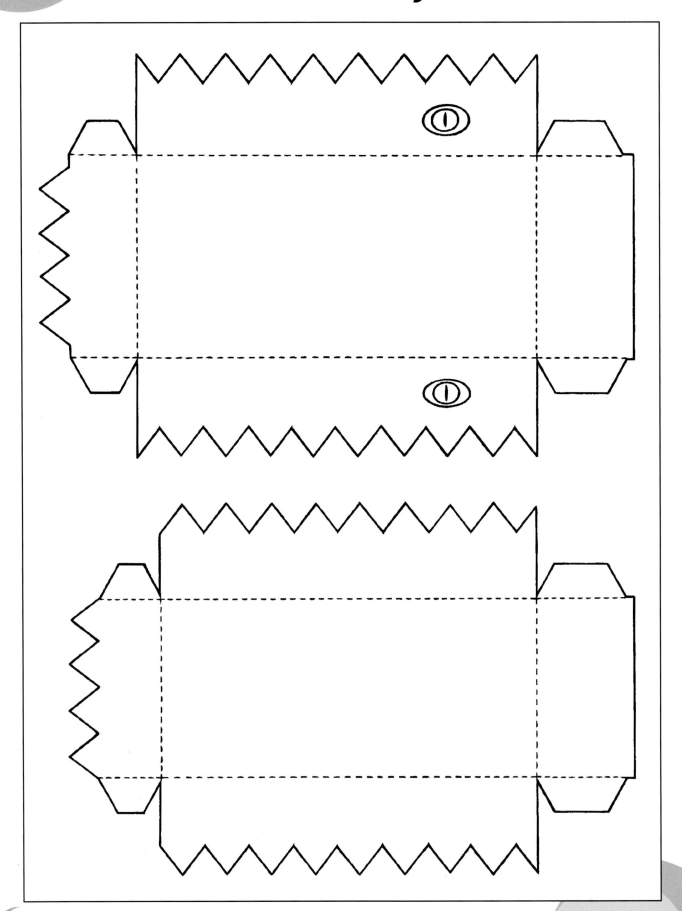

Theme 6 **Attacking a dinosaur herd**

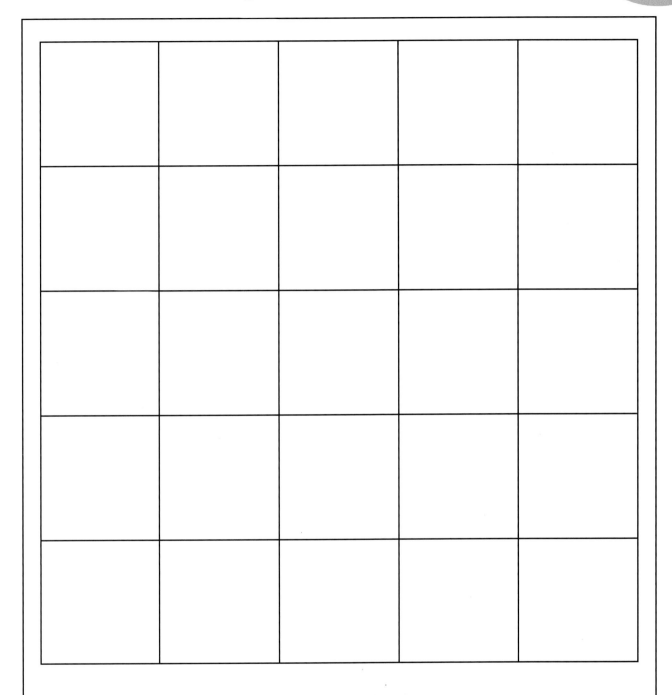

HOT TOPICS Dinosaurs

Family life

BACKGROUND

Dinosaurs laid eggs. The smallest were approximately 2.5cm long, while the largest were 30cm long and 25cm wide.

Small dinosaurs might have laid eggs in a way similar to birds, but large dinosaurs would have had to let their eggs drop from a considerable height. Some scientists think that these dinosaurs might have had an egg tube, similar to turtles, down which eggs could have been lowered to the ground.

Many dinosaurs left their laid eggs but a few built nests for their eggs. In some species, the young dinosaurs left the nest as soon as they hatched; in others, such as Maiasaura (the 'good mother lizard'), the young stayed in the nest and were fed by their mother.

It is thought that herbivorous dinosaurs kept in touch by making sounds as they moved through their habitat. Lambeosaurids had head crests through which an air tube ran. It is thought that these dinosaurs blew into their air tubes to make sounds.

Although fossil dinosaur skin has been found, showing that it had scales, there is no hint of the colour. Dinosaur colours are often based on observations of animals that are alive today. For example, some anole lizards become brightly coloured when defending their territory.

As a dinosaur bone thickened, it formed annular growth rings like those in trees. The rate of growth of a species of dinosaur is found by gathering bones of different ages and finding their masses. The mass and age of the different bones are plotted on a graph to find out how individuals in the species grew up.

Lesson 1 (Ages 5–7)
Dinosaur eggs
The children dig out a model nest and examine a nest with eggs. They make a model of a baby dinosaur in an egg.

Lesson 2 (Ages 7–9)
Communicating with dinosaurs
The children discover that some dinosaurs had hollow crests which they probably used to make sounds. They research colours of dinosaurs, reptiles and birds and make a ferocious dinosaur mask.

Lesson 3 (Ages 9–11)
Dinosaur growth
The children plot the data on the growth of a dinosaur on a graph and ask questions about it.

Notes on photocopiables
Dinosaur eggs (page 61)
This sheet shows a picture of Maiasaura at her nest. The children could colour it in later. There is also a flow diagram showing how to make a Plasticine egg containing a baby dinosaur.

Dinosaur mask (page 62)
The mask is loosely based on the ceratopsids, to which Triceratops belongs. It is thought that the frills could have been brightly coloured.

Growth of a dinosaur (page 63)
The data is loosely based on the growth of Apatosaurus. The children should see that the graph is S-shaped, similar to the growth of mammals. The answers to the questions in the lesson are: *When did growth begin to speed up?* (After 5 years.) *What was the mass at six years of age?* (3000kg.) *What was the dinosaur's mass at age 16?* (25000kg.) *How old was the dinosaur when it stopped growing?* (15 years.)

PHOTOGRAPH © NATURAL HISTORY MUSEUM

HOT TOPICS Dinosaurs

Lesson 1 Dinosaur eggs

Resources and preparation
- Make copies of page 61, 'Dinosaur eggs', for each group.
- Prepare a model dinosaur nest, comprising of a bowl of dry sand in which up to six table tennis balls (eggs) have been buried, plus a large tray to hold the bowl.
- You will need two spoons and two one-inch paint brushes with soft hairs, a metre rule or tape measure and chalk, and a large lump of Plasticine for each group.
- An outdoor space is also required.
- For the Extension, you will need an egg and a bowl or jar of vinegar.
- This lesson can be adapted as part of your Dinosaur Day.

What to do
- Show the children the picture of Maiasaura looking after its nest. Tell them that nests can be found by very careful digging that doesn't destroy the eggs.
- Present the class with the model nest and ask for two volunteers to 'dig' out the eggs using the brushes and spoons. Encourage the children to predict how many eggs are in the nest.
- Let two children dig until the first egg is found, then let two more children have a go, and so on. (The sand can be moved from the bowl to the tray.) Count all the eggs that have been retrieved and see who

predicted the correct number.
- Outside, mark out a circle that is two metres in diameter. Tell the children that this is the size of the nest produced by the dinosaur shown on the photocopiable sheet. Draw some ovals about 20cm long in a ring inside the 'nest' and tell the children that this is how Maiasaura arranged her eggs.
- Explain that baby dinosaurs grow inside eggs like the chicks of birds. Show the children how to make a model baby dinosaur in its egg. Shape two lumps of Plasticine into hollow ovals, and another piece into the shape of a baby dinosaur, as shown on the sheet. Hinge the two halves of the 'egg' at one side, and place the baby dinosaur inside. The children can then open and close their egg to reveal the baby dinosaur.

Extension
Tell more confident learners that over time the inside of an egg turns to fossil but the shell remains the same. Palaeontologists remove the shell by placing the egg in a weak acid. Demonstrate this by placing a real egg in vinegar and leave it for three days. By then the shell should have dissolved leaving a leathery skin containing the rest of the egg. The dissolved shell enables the contents to be examined.

PHOTOGRAPH © PETER ROWE

Lesson 2 Communicating with dinosaurs

AGES 7–9

Objectives
- To realise that dinosaurs may have communicated with sound and colours.
- To make a dinosaur mask which displays aggression.

Subject references
Art and design
Record from first-hand observation and explore ideas. (NC: KS2 1a) Select ideas to use in work. (NC: KS2 1b) Communicate observations, ideas and feelings. (NC: KS2 2c)

Resources and preparation
- Photocopy page 62, 'Dinosaur mask', for each child.
- Provide a picture of Lambeosaurus, and secondary sources showing pictures of other dinosaurs, in particular Triceratops, Torosaurus, Centrosaurus and Protoceratops, as well as present-day reptiles and birds.
- You will need empty plastic bottles of different sizes, a selection of paints and paintbrushes, string, scissors and sticky paper.
- This lesson can be adapted as part of your Dinosaur Day.

Starter
- Ask the children to think about how dinosaurs communicated with each other and with other species, for example by roaring. Tell them that there were a group of dinosaurs which had hollow crests on their heads, and show them a picture of Lambeosaurus. Explain that it is thought that these dinosaurs blew air into their crests to make sounds in order to communicate with each other.
- Give out the plastic bottles and tell the children to imagine that they are members of a herd of lambeosaurids! Ask them to blow into the bottles and listen to the sound each other is making. Ask them who are large lambeosaurids and who are small ones. (This is related, in this case, not to the children's body size but to the size of the bottle and the pitch of the note they make.)

What to do
- Explain to the children that nobody really knows what colour dinosaurs were because the colour has been lost from any skin that has been found, but it is thought that they had the colours of present-day reptiles and birds.
- Give each child a copy of the 'Dinosaur mask' photocopiable sheet and explain that its features are based on the group of dinosaurs to which Triceratops belongs. These dinosaurs had frills, which might have been highly coloured to warn other

PHOTOGRAPH © DEREK COOKNELL

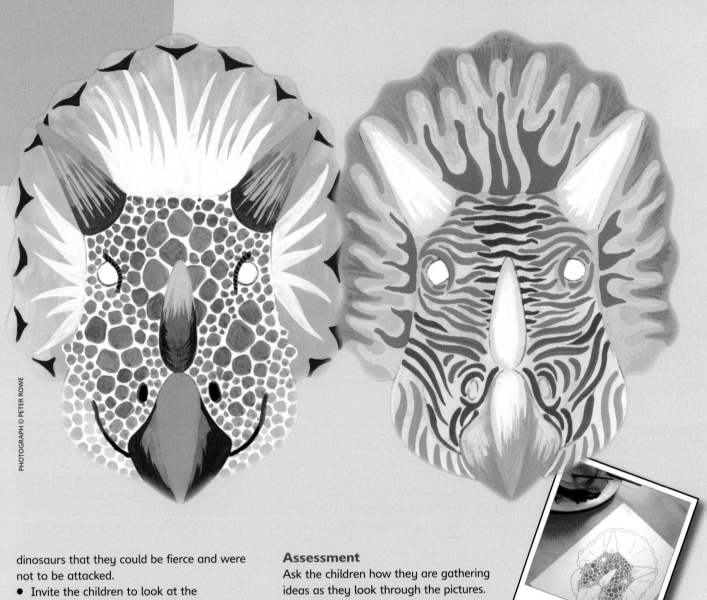

dinosaurs that they could be fierce and were not to be attacked.

- Invite the children to look at the secondary source pictures of different dinosaurs and present-day reptiles and birds, and gather ideas for colours and patterns for painting their masks. Remind them to make their dinosaur faces look ferocious!
- Let the children paint their masks. When they are dry, help the children to attach string to the back so that the masks can be held in place on their heads.
- Enjoy the different colours the children have chosen and let them make a few roars at each other.

Differentiation

- Some children may need adult help in deciding what colours and patterns to use after looking at the secondary sources.
- Encourage more confident learners to use their imagination to work out a series of sound signals between the lambeosaurids in the herd and to demonstrate these to the rest of the class. They may also like to try to make and attach horns to the mask for added realism.

Assessment

Ask the children how they are gathering ideas as they look through the pictures. As they make their masks, find out how their work is making the face look ferocious. The quality of the masks may also be assessed.

Plenary

Make a display of the masks, and identify and discuss themes for making the face look ferocious. If the activity has been divided into several sessions, more confident learners may have had time to work out some communication signals and demonstrate them to the class.

Outcomes

- The children are aware that dinosaurs probably communicated by sound.
- The children can use secondary sources to gather information and ideas.
- The children are aware that dinosaurs probably used colour in communication.

Lesson 3 Dinosaur growth

Resources and preparation
● Make copies of page 63, 'Growth of a dinosaur', for each child.
● Source a picture showing a close-up of the growth rings in a large tree trunk.

What to do
● Show the children the picture of the growth rings in a tree trunk and ask them how old they think the tree is. How can they tell? If they don't already know, explain that as the tree grows bigger another ring is formed each year. Tell the children that palaeontologists have found that dinosaur bones have growth rings in them as well, but these are tiny and can only be seen with a microscope.
● Explain that palaeontologists use the growth rings and the masses of bones (weight in kilograms) of dinosaurs of the same species, but of different ages, to work out how fast that kind of dinosaur grew and for how long it continued to grow.
● Give each child a copy of the photocopiable sheet and tell the class that the data represents the growth of a dinosaur similar to Apatosaurus. Looking at the age and weight information at the top of the sheet, ask the children to plot the data on the graph in dots and then draw lines between the points. Which letter of the alphabet do the children think the line on the graph looks like?
● Ask the children questions about the graph to develop their data-finding and interpretation skills. For example: *when did growth begin to speed up? What was the mass of the dinosaur at six years of age? What was the dinosaur's mass at age 16? How old was the dinosaur when it stopped growing?*

Extension
Invite the children to collect data about the growth of kittens or puppies, and to plot them on a graph in the same way. They should see that these mammals have the same S-shaped growth patterns as dinosaurs had.

Did you know?
A full grown Ultrasaurus weighed the same as a herd of twenty elephants.

ILLUSTRATION © LASZLO VERES/BEEHIVE ILLUSTRATION

HOT TOPICS Dinosaurs

Theme 7 Dinosaur eggs

- **Maiasaura at her nest**

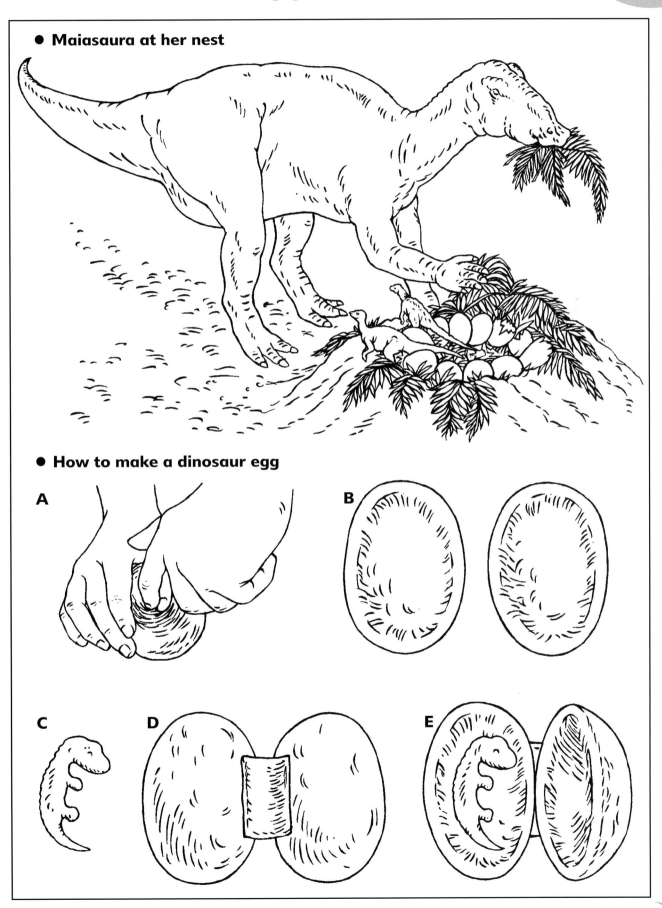

- **How to make a dinosaur egg**

A

B

C

D

E

HOT TOPICS Dinosaurs

Theme 7 Dinosaur mask

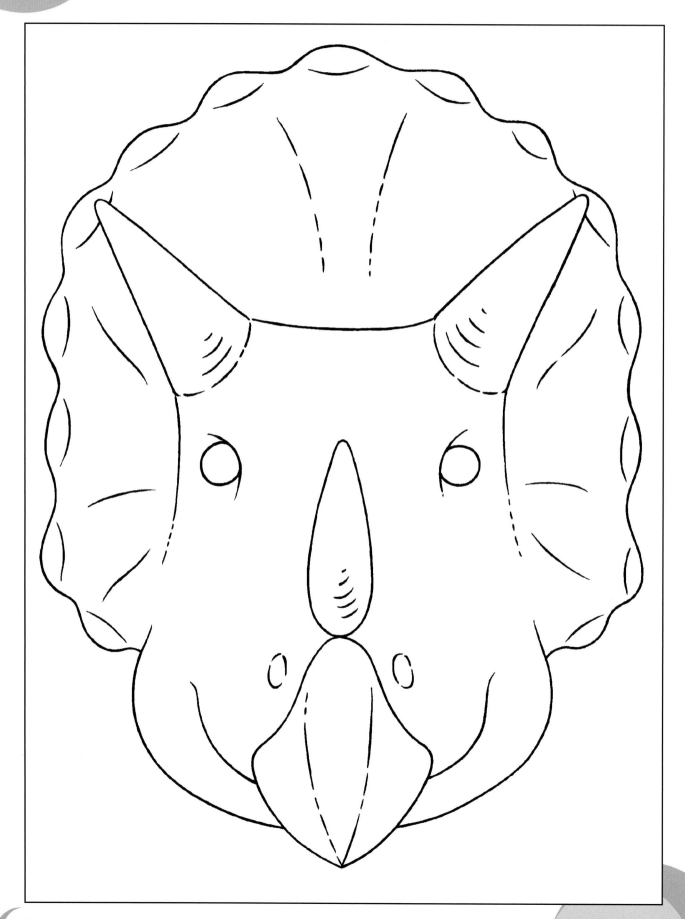

Theme 7 Growth of a dinosaur

Age (years)	Mass (kg)
0	0
2	500
5	1000
7	5000
8	10 000
9	15 000
10	20 000
12	24 000
15	26 000
17	26 000

Mass (kg)

30 000 —

25 000 —

20 000 —

15 000 —

10 000 —

5 000 —

0 —

1 2 3 4 5 6 7 8 9 10 11 12 13 14 15 16 17

Age (years)

The Age of dinosaurs

BACKGROUND

The geological period before the age of the dinosaurs was the Permian era. At the end of this period a massive extinction occurred, far greater than the one in which the dinosaurs died out. It is thought that this earlier extinction occurred when continents fused together to form an enormous land mass. This in turn led to a huge ocean being formed in which there was a weak circulation of currents. The water became stagnant and released so much carbon dioxide that the Earth became hot. It was 20 million years into the Triassic period before life began to develop rapidly again.

During the age of the dinosaurs, the continents split apart again and brought about further climate change. At the beginning of the age, the major plants were mosses, horsetails and ferns. Coniferous trees developed and, in the Cretaceous period, the first flowering plants appeared. Dinosaurs developed towards the end of the Triassic period. Only a few kinds have been found from then, but in the periods that followed some dinosaurs became extinct and other species developed. Not all 'familiar' dinosaurs were alive at the same time.

Dinosaur fossils were misinterpreted until the early 19th century when comparisons were made between the fossils and animal bones. This is when the dinosaurs were recognised as a distinct group.

THE CONTENTS

Lesson 1 (Ages 5–7)
Dinosaur world
The children learn a song which explains how dinosaurs behaved and came to an end. You could link it with Theme 9 Lesson 1.

Lesson 2 (Ages 7–9)
Dinosaur times
The children assemble dinosaurs and other animals into three dinosaur time periods.

Lesson 3 (Ages 9–11)
Discovering dinosaurs
The children find out about early discoveries of dinosaurs.

Notes on photocopiables
We are the dinosaurs (page 69)
Nobody is really sure what hit the Earth; it could have been an asteroid or a comet. 'Comet' has been used here to fit the tune. There is a little poetic license in the last line as the name Brontosaurus is no longer used (see page 8), although it is still used by the general public. The music is a simple piano piece, with an easy melody and 'walking' bassline. It can work with the piano and children singing, or with recorder players. If tuned percussion, such as the xylophone, is used, only F and C are needed. The other notes may be removed, or coloured stickers placed on the relevant bars and the notes in the book given the same colour. A drum could beat throughout or the children can clap along. Cymbals and other noisy instruments can bring the song to a close.

The times of the dinosaurs (page 70)
Time periods: Triassic (248m – 213m years ago); Jurassic (213m – 144m); Cretaceous (144m – 65m).
Animals alive in these times: archaeopteryx – one of the first birds; ichthyornis – a bird; ichthyosaur – a fish-like reptile; plesiosaur – an aquatic reptile; pterosaur – a winged reptile.

Discovering dinosaurs (page 71)
Answers: 1) 63; 2) It had wings; 3a) 72 years, b) 62 years, c) 88 years; 4) Yes. If she had gone the other way or the stone had been turned over she would never have seen it; 5) A little under half their size; 6) Mantell.

PHOTOGRAPH © KFAWCETT, STOCK.XCHNG

Lesson 1 Dinosaur world

Resources and preparation
● Make a copy of 'We are the dinosaurs' on page 69 for each child.
● Make or find suitable items for a costume for the dinosaur wizard (to be worn by one of the children). Alternatively, make two witch and wizard face masks by adapting the dinosaur mask on photocopiable page 62.
● Provide musical instruments (optional variations: see Notes on photocopiables on page 64).
● You will also need a beach ball.
● For the Extension, gather a large deep tray, compost, plenty of moss, small ferns and conifers, rocks and pebbles, and the children's model dinosaurs.
● This lesson can be adapted to be part of your Dinosaur Day.

What to do
● Ask the children to imagine that there is a wizard or witch who can turn people into dinosaurs. *What would this magical person look like?* Ask the children to suggest a costume, and try to provide it for one volunteer. Alternatively, invite two children to be a wizard and witch, where one says the introduction and the other invites everyone to join in at the end of the song.
● Tell the children that they are going to learn a special song that the dinosaur wizard and his dinosaurs sing. Go through the song with the class. Ask the children to demonstrate some ideas about how they could provide movements for each verse. In the last verse, a child can throw a beach ball into the air when the class sings the line *Comet crashed...*
● Rehearse the performance so that it is ready for your Dinosaur Day as suggested on pages 6 and 7.

Extension
Invite the children to set up a habitat for their model dinosaurs. Help them to lay potting compost in a tray and cover it with moss. Sink pots of small ferns and conifers into the compost, and place rocks and dinosaurs on the top. Encourage the children to make a drawing of their dinosaur world.

PHOTOGRAPH © PETER ROWE. DINOSAUR MODELS © EARLY LEARNING CENTRE

AGES 5–7

Objectives
● To learn and perform a song.
● To set up a dinosaur habitat.

Subject references
Music
● Use voice expressively in singing songs. (NC: KS1 1a)
● Explore and express ideas and feelings about music using movement. (NC: KS1 3a)
● Listen with concentration and internalise and recall sounds with increasing aural memory. (NC: KS1 4a)

Lesson 2 Dinosaur times

Resources and preparation
- Make copies of page 70, 'The times of the dinosaurs', one for each child.
- You will need rulers, scissors, glue and paper.
- Provide secondary information sources on the Triassic, Jurassic and Cretaceous periods.

Starter
- Remind the children about peoples from a very long time ago that they have studied in history, such as the Romans, the Egyptians or the Ancient Greeks. Tell them that we measure back in thousands of years to find the times when these people lived. Explain that we must measure back in millions of years to the time when dinosaurs lived.
- Invite the children to look at their rulers and imagine that each millimetre represents a million years. This means that each centimetre represents ten million years. Give the following instructions to the children so that everyone understands when each time period started and finished (they could mark each one on their rulers as a reminder):
  - Imagine that zero is the present day and count on to 6.5cm. This represents the end of the age of the dinosaurs.
  - Count on to 22.5cm. This represents the beginning of the age of the dinosaurs.
  - Move on to 24.8cm. This is the beginning of a time called the Triassic period.
  - Move back to 21.3cm. This represents the end of the Triassic period and the beginning of the Jurassic period.
  - Move back again to 14.4 cm. This represents the end of the Jurassic period and the beginning of the Cretaceous period, which ended back at 6.5cm – 65 million years ago.
- Explain to the children that they have already learned a lot about dinosaurs, but they haven't yet learned when each one lived. Now they are going to find out!

What to do
- Tell the children that they are going to group dinosaurs and other animals into the three time periods: the Triassic, the Jurassic and the Cretaceous.
- Give the children the photocopiable sheet and ask them to cut out the names of the animals with their time periods.
- Using the information already discussed in the Starter, ask the children to group the

Did you know?
Some of the first dinosaurs were small - only two to three metres long.

The Triassic Period	**The Jurassic Period**
225 million years ago	213 million years ago

animals according to time period and to glue them onto a sheet of paper. Tell them to arrange the time periods in chronological order, starting with the Triassic.

● Ask the children questions about the information they have ordered, for example: *Did Diplodocus live at the same time as Stegosaurus? Did Tyrannosaurus live at the same time as Stegosaurus? Did Velociraptor live at the same time as Triceratops? Did Plateosaurus and Brachiosaurus live at the same time?*

● Ask the children to use secondary sources to find out more about the dinosaurs in each age and to make a drawing of each one on a separate piece of paper, for display later. They should caption the drawing with the dinosaur's name and the period in which it lived, and record the size of the dinosaur. Ensure that the children also identify the animals featured which are not dinosaurs.

Differentiation
● Some children may need help to sort out the animals. Encourage them to select one animal from each age to find out about.
● Extend children by inviting them to find out about other dinosaurs that have

featured in this book. These include Ceratosaurus, Cetiosaurus, Gallimimus, Kentrosaurus, Lambeosaurus, Nodosaurus, Tenontosaurus and Troodon.

Assessment
Assess the children by the ease at which they sort out the dinosaurs and animals into a timeline and answer the questions. They can also be assessed on the quality of their research.

Plenary
Set up a display board for the three ages of the dinosaurs. Invite the children to pin their pictures of dinosaurs in the appropriate age. Ask them to show you which animals they consider not to be dinosaurs, and look for the ichthyosaur, plesiosaur, pterosaur, ichtyhornis and archaeopteryx.

Outcomes
● The children can arrange the dinosaurs on a timeline.
● They can use secondary sources to find out about dinosaurs.
● They can identify some animals from the age of dinosaurs which are not dinosaurs.

The Cretaceous Period

144 million
years ago

65 million
years ago

ILLUSTRATION © LASZLO VERES/BEEHIVE ILLUSTRATION

Lesson 3 Discovering dinosaurs

Resources and preparation
● Make copies of page 71, 'Discovering dinosaurs', for each child.
● For the Extension, blank invitations, cardboard and craft materials and tools, Victorian costumes are required.
● This lesson can be developed to form part of your Dinosaur Day.

What to do
● Ask the children to tell you any information that they have found out so far about how dinosaurs were discovered. Keep a record of their ideas on the board to refer back to later.
● Give the children time to read through the text on the photocopiable sheet, helping them with difficult vocabulary as appropriate.
● Ask the children to answer the questions at the bottom of the photocopiable sheet.
● When the children have finished, discuss what they have written and share the answers with the whole class. See Notes on photocopiables on page 64 for the answers.
● Compare the children's ideas noted on the board at the start of the session with the account given on the photocopiable sheet. Ask the children in what ways were their ideas similar to what really happened, and in what ways were they different from them.

Extension
● This session could be integrated neatly with history work on the Victorians. The children can find out what happened in Victorian England when the name 'Dinosauria' was introduced. For example, a man named Richard Owen worked with the sculptor Benjamin Waterhouse Hawkins in making life-size concrete models of dinosaurs. They were set up in Sydenham Park in London, and are still there today. The models served to introduce ordinary people to dinosaurs and helped to generate the fascination with them that exists to this day.
● To celebrate the setting up of the models, Owen organised a dinner for 22 people inside an open-topped model of Iguanodon. Invitations to the dinner were sent out on cards with a picture of a pterosaur on them. The text of the invitation was written in the animal's wing.
● Encourage the children to research this event and help them to build a large model of the side of a dinosaur from cardboard. They can then send out invitations, set up chairs and tables behind the side of the dinosaur model, dress in Victorian clothes and have a Victorian meal.

PHOTOGRAPH © NATURAL HISTORY MUSEUM

Theme 8 We are the dinosaurs

Dinosaur wizard says to children: Hocus Pocus Diplodocus, Leave your chores be dinosaurs.'

The children sing:

1.We are the di-no-saurs stamp-ing on the

ground. E-ven though you're far a-w-ay, you can hear our sound.

2) We are the dinosaurs,
   Big as big can be,
   Striding out across the plain,
   For everyone to see.

3) We are the dinosaurs,
   Roaring in the air,
   Hollering and bellowing,
   Giving everyone a scare.

4) We were the dinosaurs,
   We lived long ago,
   Comet crashed, Earth trashed,
   Killed us all just so.

Dinosaur wizard says to the audience: 'Come along and join our chorus,
                                          Everyone be a Brontosaurus.'

Everyone sings the song from the beginning again.

Music by Sally-Anne Riley, Words by Peter Riley

MUSIC SET BY SALLY SCOTT

Theme 8 The times of the dinosaurs

Oviraptor	Cretaceous
Diplodocus	Jurassic
Velociraptor	Cretaceous
Coelophysis	Triassic
Stegosaurus	Jurassic
Ichthyosaur	Triassic
Triceratops	Cretaceous
Apatosaurus	Jurassic
Plateosaurus	Triassic
Ankylosaurus	Cretaceous
Archaeopteryx	Jurassic
Tyrannosaurus	Cretaceous
Plesiosaur	Jurassic
Maiasaura	Cretaceous
Allosaurus	Jurassic
Ichthyornis	Cretaceous
Brachiosaurus	Jurassic
Pterosaur	Cretaceous

Theme 8 Discovering dinosaurs

Humans have been on Earth for approximately two million years. Dinosaurs died out around 65 million years ago, so nobody has ever seen a living dinosaur. Everything we know about dinosaurs, we have learned from their fossils. At first, however, people did not recognise the fossils for what they were.

In China, people thought that fossil dinosaur bones were dragon bones. In Ancient Greece, people thought that an animal called the griffin existed. It had a beak, a long body with four legs and two wings. It is possible they had the idea for this animal from dinosaur fossils of Protoceratops, which had four legs, no wings but a beak and a body two metres long.

William Buckland (1784–1856) was a geologist who examined a large fossil jaw with teeth in it and thought that it belonged to a giant extinct lizard. He reported his observations in 1824 and named the animal 'Megalosaurus', which meant 'great lizard'. Gideon Mantell (1790–1852) was a doctor and geologist. His wife Mary Ann used to accompany him when he visited patients in their homes. On one such visit in 1822, she went for a walk down a lane while her husband tended his patient. She saw a shiny object glinting from a rock in a pile of stones being used to repair the road. When she showed the object to her husband, he recognised it as a tooth. He spent a long time comparing the tooth with other teeth and eventually, in 1825, he discovered that the tooth was very similar to the tooth of a lizard called an iguana, but there was one big difference. The fossil tooth was 20 times the size of the lizard tooth! He thought he had discovered a giant lizard and called it 'Iguanodon', which means 'iguana tooth'.

In 1832, Mantell discovered another dinosaur fossil. He named it 'Hylaeosaurus', which means 'Wealden Lizard' after the Weald region of England in which it was found. This animal was about four metres long.

Richard Owen (1804–1892) compared the Megalosaurus, Iguanadon and Hylaeosaurus fossils with the bones of other reptiles and decided that they were not lizards but a group of their own. In 1842, he named this group the Dinosauria from which we get the word 'dinosaur'. It means 'fearfully great lizard'.

1. How many million years passed between the end of the dinosaurs and humans developing on the planet?

2. How was a griffin different from Protoceratops?

3. How long did (a) Buckland, (b) Mantell, (c) Owen live?

4. Do you think Mary Ann Mantel was lucky to discover a fossil?
Explain your answer.

5. It is now known that Megalosaurus and Iguanadon were nine metres long.
How does the size of Hylaeosaurus compare?

6. Queen Victoria began her reign in 1837.
Which dinosaur discoverer died in the 15th year of her reign?

The end of the dinosaurs

BACKGROUND

There have been many theories on what caused the extinction of the dinosaurs. One is that the mammals that were developing at the same time ate their eggs; another is that they were killed by a plague. At the moment, however, two events are thought to have contributed to their extinction.

The first is that the plate of the Earth's crust carrying the Indian continent was pushing strongly into the plate carrying Asia. This resulted in many huge volcanoes forming and erupting. The ash covered vast areas of land and wiped out the life there. Clouds of gas moved around the planet and reduced the sunlight.

Secondly, a ten-kilometre asteroid or comet hit Earth. A great amount of heat was generated by the impact, and hot rock and dust were thrown many kilometres into the air. As the hot rocks came down they caused massive fires and killed everything beneath them. Dust clouds formed, which cut out more light. The clouds remained for many years and the lack of light killed most of the plants. The herbivorous dinosaurs did not have enough food to eat and so they died. The carnivorous dinosaurs had nothing to eat and died too.

Other animals, however, including mammals, birds and insects, survived and developed more species when the clouds cleared and plants began to grow again

Careful study of the bones of some dinosaurs and birds show that they could be related. Many palaeontologists believe that birds are really dinosaurs with feathers and as long as birds are alive, the age of dinosaurs is not really over.

THE CONTENTS

Lesson 1 (Ages 5–7)
Plants and light
The children see how volcanoes produce clouds. They find out that objects can break and scatter on impact. They realise that both an asteroid and volcanoes could make a cloud to cut out light. Then, they investigate the effect of light on plants.

Lesson 2 (Ages 7–9)
Volcanoes and a space rock
The children find that evidence for extinction comes from the distribution of the fossils in the ground. They investigate the way a model volcano scatters material, and how a model asteroid scatters material on impact.

Lesson 3 (Ages 9–11)
The end of the dinosaurs
The children look at a model of the spread of the effects of the impact. They locate places on a map and put them in the order in which the impact would have affected them.

Notes on photocopiables
Plants and light (page 77)
The pictures show the set-up for the experiment. The children can record their observations after one week, and again after two weeks.

Volcanoes and a space rock (page 78)
A model volcano is made to assess how far the ash and debris from a volcano would spread. The sheet shows the layout for an impact experiment.

The effect of the impact (page 79)
This sheet shows a world map and questions for children to answer about what would have happened after the impact of a comet or asteroid.
The answers are:
2) New York, Rio de Janeiro, London, Cape Town, Karachi, Calcutta; 4) Hadrosaurus, Triceratops, Aegyptosaurus, Tyrannosaurus.

PHOTOGRAPH © DIGITAL VISION LTD

Lesson 1 Plants and light

Resources and preparation
● Make a copy of page 77, 'Plants and light', for each child
● Provide plant pots, compost and seeds, (for example mustard seeds), a measuring cylinder, and a cardboard box.
● Source pictures of volcanoes erupting, and pictures of people playing with snowballs.

What to do
● Show the children a picture of a volcano erupting. Point out the huge dark cloud it makes. Explain that at the end of the age of the dinosaurs there were many huge volcanoes erupting and making clouds, which covered large parts of the Earth.
● Now show a picture of people throwing snowballs and talk about the snow spreading out after it hits someone or something. Compare this to an asteroid hitting the Earth: bits of it spread out and form a cloud which covers the Earth.
● Ask the children how they think this darkness might have affected the dinosaurs. Prompt them to think about how it affected plants, and introduce the plant experiment.

● Explain to the class that they are going to test how well plants grow with and without light. Let the children sow some seeds and when the seedlings start to grow, keep one set of seeds in natural light and the others in a cardboard box. Each batch of seeds must receive the same amount of water and be kept at the same temperature to make the test fair.
● After a week, let the children examine both batches of seedlings and draw the results on their photocopiable sheet. Repeat after two weeks. The seedlings in the light should be green and sturdy. The seedlings in the dark should be pale and spindly.
● Ask the children how the clouds/darkness affected the plants and look for an answer about the darkness killing them.

Extension
If the children have made a dinosaur habitat (see Theme 8 Lesson 1, page 65), ask them to remove the plants. *What will happen to the dinosaurs now that there are no plants to eat?* The children might show this visually by laying the dinosaurs down or removing them from the habitat.

ILLUSTRATION © LASZLO VERES/BEEHIVE ILLUSTRATION

Lesson 2 Volcanoes and a space rock

AGES 7–9

Objectives
● To see how the action of volcanoes may have led to the extinction of the dinosaurs.
● To see how the impact of an asteroid or comet may have led to the extinction of the dinosaurs.

Subject references
Science
● Make a fair test. (NC: KS2 Sc1 2d)
● Use simple equipment appropriately and take action to control risks. (NC: KS2 Sc1 2e)
English
● Imagine and explore ideas, focusing on creative uses of language and how to interest the reader. (NC: KS2 En3 9a)

Resources and preparation
● Set up a bowl of sand with cut-up card dinosaur skeletons from photocopiable page 21 scattered in the bottom 6cm of sand. Above this put about another 10cm of sand.
● Find pictures of a volcano erupting, showing the land surrounding it covered in ash.
● Make copies of page 78, 'Volcanoes and a space rock'.
● You will also need a large bowl or bucket of water, a plastic funnel and plastic tube, two tablespoons, a plastic bowl full of plain flour, a Plasticine ball approximately 1.5cm across and one approximately 3cm across.
● Place a small table in a large outdoor space.
● Also clear a table or space on the floor, and have a brush or cloth for wiping it.
● Have safety goggles to hand.
● This lesson can be adapted as part of your Dinosaur Day.

Starter
● Remind the children that we know about dinosaurs from the fossils they left behind. When fossils form they become enclosed in rock and then more rock settles on top of them. If there are no fossils in a certain layer of rock, it indicates that the animals were not alive at that time.
● Give the class the bowl of sand containing the dinosaur skeletons. Ask for two volunteers to be palaeontologists and to dig, using the spoons, to look for fossils. They will have to dig for a long time before they reach the dinosaurs and then they will find a large number of bones at once, and more as they dig deeper.
● When they have found several, remind the class that for quite a depth no fossils were found and then a large number were discovered together. This indicates that all the dinosaurs were wiped out at a certain time in the past. Since that discovery, scientists have looked for an explanation for their extinction.

What to do
● Show the children a picture of an erupting volcano and notice the clouds it produces. Point out the ash that has settled on the land and explain that the material from a volcano can spread out over a wide area.

Did you know?
Crocodiles lived in Dinosaur times, but survived the mass extinction.

PHOTOGRAPH © PETER ROWE

HOT TOPICS Dinosaurs

- Tell the children that you are going to create a model volcano. Show them the materials/equipment and explain that when someone blows on the tube it creates pressure inside the volcano, which moves the liquid upwards, just as liquid rock inside a volcano is forced out by pressure from deep in the ground.
- Set up the experiment on a small table outside. Fill the bowl with water and place a plastic funnel upside down so that the tube of the funnel is above the water, and the cone of the funnel is below the water line. Then feed the plastic tube into the cone end of the funnel, keeping hold of the other end of the tube to blow in to.
- Encourage the children to notice the dry area around the volcano and then blow into the tube so that the water is forced through the plastic funnel.
- Let the children notice where the water falls and ask them to imagine a volcano millions of times the size of the model sending out material when it erupted. Can the children understand how the whole world can be affected by volcano eruptions?
- Back inside, show the children the bowl of flour and explain that this represents the site of an asteroid impact. Hold up the 1.5cm Plasticine ball and explain that this is a small asteroid.
- Place the bowl of flour on a clear table top and ask the children what might happen when you throw it lightly into the flour. Tell the children to stand well back as you gently throw the Plasticine ball into the bowl. Ask the children to sketch the fallout of flour on the table in the appropriate space on the photocopiable sheet.
- Ask the children to predict what might happen if you use a larger 'asteroid' and show them the 3cm Plasticine ball. Move the children further back and repeat the previous experiment with the larger 'asteroid'. Again, ask the children to sketch the fallout of flour.

- Encourage the children to think about what they have seen and to write an account of what it might have been like for a dinosaur as the volcanoes erupted and the space rock hit the Earth.

Differentiation
- Ask less confident learners to illustrate the conditions for dinosaurs as the volcanoes erupted and space rock hit. They could add labels to their drawing or write a few lines underneath to describe what is happening.
- Encourage more confident learners to use secondary sources and read accounts of the extinction of the dinosaurs.

Assessment
Assess the children on their drawings of the fallout from the model asteroid impacts. They could also be assessed on the quality of their written or pictorial work.

Plenary
Ask the children to imagine that they are a herd of dinosaurs feeding in a forest when a volcano erupts. Tell them that they manage to get away from the fallen ash but then see the asteroid or comet in the sky. Can they explain what happened next? Some children may say they were hit with the space rock, but focus on the effect of the fallout. Explain that there was also an earthquake and high winds from the shock of the impact.

Outcome
The children understand how volcanoes and the impact of an asteroid or comet contributed to the extinction of the dinosaurs.

HOT TOPICS Dinosaurs

Lesson 3 The end of the dinosaurs

Resources and preparation
● Make a copy of page 79, 'The effect of the impact', for each child.
● Set up a large shallow tray containing water and a pebble.
● You will also need an atlas or globe.

What to do
● Ask the children to imagine that the surface of the water in the tray represents the surface of the Earth, and the pebble represents the asteroid or comet.
● Tell the children to watch the water carefully. Drop the pebble in the centre of the water and let the children see the ripples spread across the water. Explain to the children that when the space rock hit the Earth, earthquakes and strong winds spread out from the point of impact across the Earth.
● Give the children the photocopiable sheet and ask them to look closely at the map. Can they find the UK? Can they find it in an atlas or on a globe?
● Now ask the children to work through the tasks and answer the questions on the sheet, marking their answers on the map on the photocopiable sheet. When they have finished, invite them to share their answers with the rest of the class. See Notes on photocopiables on page 72 for the answers.

Extension
Tell the children that many scientists believe that birds are really feathered dinosaurs and so perhaps the age of the dinosaurs is not over. Ask the children to look out for these dinosaurs on their way to and from school. Encourage them to record the features of the birds they see and to identify them in bird books. *How many different dinosaurs live in the neighbourhood around the school?*

Did you know?
Some dinosaurs had wishbones like birds. This shows how dinosaurs and birds may be related.

PHOTOGRAPH © EMILYB. STOCK.XCHNG

HOT TOPICS Dinosaurs

Theme 9 **Plants and light**

After 1 week

After 1 week

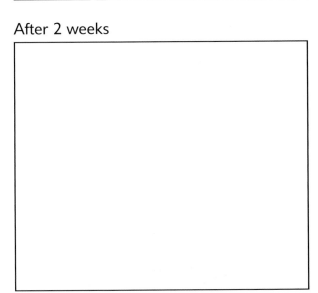

After 2 weeks

Theme 9 Volcanoes and a space rock

Volcanoes

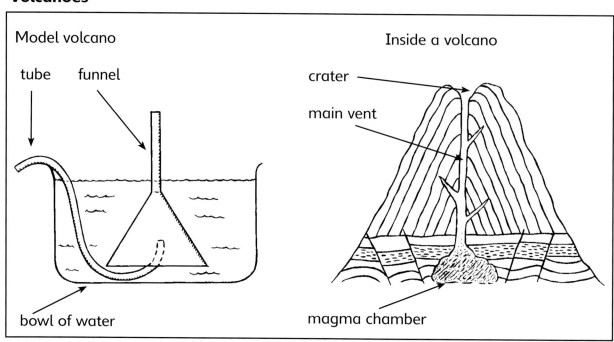

Model volcano

tube   funnel

bowl of water

Inside a volcano

crater

main vent

magma chamber

Space rock – an asteroid or comet

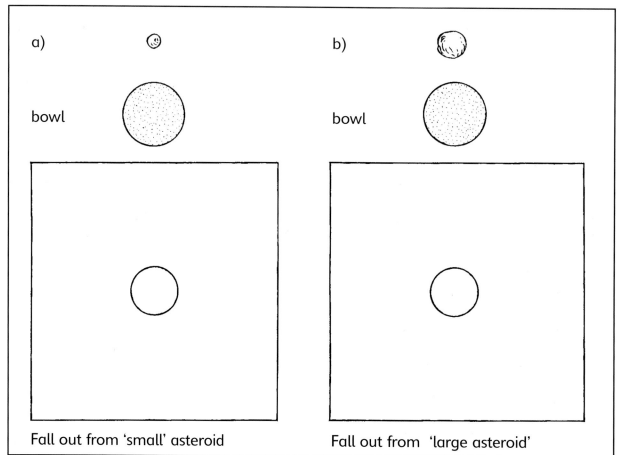

a)

bowl

Fall out from 'small' asteroid

b)

bowl

Fall out from 'large asteroid'

Theme 9 The effect of the impact

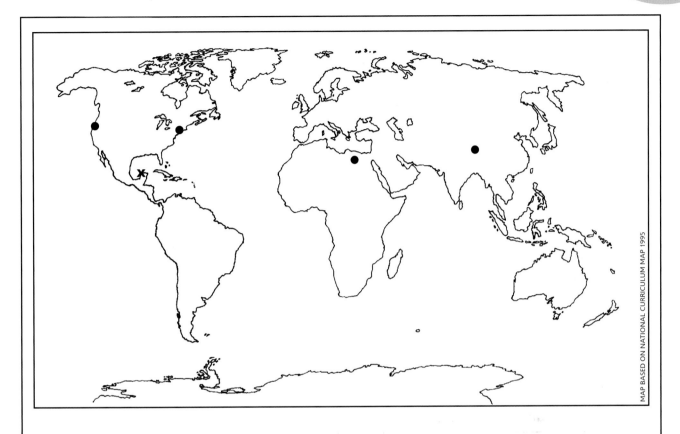

MAP BASED ON NATIONAL CURRICULUM MAP 1995

1. Use an atlas to find the location of London, New York, Cape Town, Karachi, Calcutta and Rio de Janeiro. Mark their positions on the map above and label them.

2. The impact occurred at the Yucatan peninsula which is marked with 'X'. If it occurred today, in which order would the cities be affected?

_____

_____

3. The dots represent the sites of fossils found from dinosaurs which were alive when the impact occurred. Use an atlas to locate these sites, and add the following labels to the map:
A) Tyrannosaurus – Mongolia.
B) Triceratops – west coast of North America
C) Aegyptosaurus – Egypt
D) Hadrosaurus – east coast of North America

4. In which order were these dinosaurs affected by the impact?

_____

_____

 TOPICS Dinosaurs

SCHOLASTIC

In this series:

ISBN 0-439-94510-0
ISBN 978-0439-94510-3

ISBN 0-439-94552-6
ISBN 978-0439-94552-3

To find out more, call: 0845 603 9091
or visit www.scholastic.co.uk